CAMBRIDGE LIBRARY COLLECTION

Books of enduring scholarly value

Religion

For centuries, scripture and theology were the focus of prodigious amounts of scholarship and publishing, dominated in the English-speaking world by the work of Protestant Christians. Enlightenment philosophy and science, anthropology, ethnology and the colonial experience all brought new perspectives, lively debates and heated controversies to the study of religion and its role in the world, many of which continue to this day. This series explores the editing and interpretation of religious texts, the history of religious ideas and institutions, and not least the encounter between religion and science.

More Worlds Than One

Sir David Brewster (1781–1868) was a distinguished scientist and inventor who frequently turned the results of his research to practical ends; his work on the diffraction of light, for example, led to his developing improved reflectors for lighthouses and inventing two popular Victorian toys, the stereoscope and the kaleidoscope. He was also active as the editor of the Edinburgh Magazine and the Edinburgh Encyclopaedia (1808–30) and contributed to the seventh and eighth editions of the Encyclopaedia Britannica, as well as writing many articles for a variety of philosophical and scientific journals. He was deeply religious, and in More Worlds Than One (1854) he set out to counter the arguments against extra-terrestrial life in William Whewell's recently published Of the Plurality of Worlds (also reissued in this series), urging that Whewell's 'extraordinary doctrine' was wrong on scientific grounds.

Cambridge University Press has long been a pioneer in the reissuing of out-of-print titles from its own backlist, producing digital reprints of books that are still sought after by scholars and students but could not be reprinted economically using traditional technology. The Cambridge Library Collection extends this activity to a wider range of books which are still of importance to researchers and professionals, either for the source material they contain, or as landmarks in the history of their academic discipline.

Drawing from the world-renowned collections in the Cambridge University Library, and guided by the advice of experts in each subject area, Cambridge University Press is using state-of-the-art scanning machines in its own Printing House to capture the content of each book selected for inclusion. The files are processed to give a consistently clear, crisp image, and the books finished to the high quality standard for which the Press is recognised around the world. The latest print-on-demand technology ensures that the books will remain available indefinitely, and that orders for single or multiple copies can quickly be supplied.

The Cambridge Library Collection will bring back to life books of enduring scholarly value (including out-of-copyright works originally issued by other publishers) across a wide range of disciplines in the humanities and social sciences and in science and technology.

More Worlds Than One

The Creed of the Philosopher and the Hope of the Christian

David Brewster

CAMBRIDGE UNIVERSITY PRESS

Cambridge, New York, Melbourne, Madrid, Cape Town, Singapore,
São Paolo, Delhi, Dubai, Tokyo

Published in the United States of America by Cambridge University Press, New York

www.cambridge.org
Information on this title: www.cambridge.org/9781108004169

This edition first published 1854
This digitally printed version 2009

ISBN 978-1-108-00416-9 Paperback

MORE WORLDS THAN ONE

THE CREED OF THE PHILOSOPHER

AND THE HOPE OF THE CHRISTIAN.

BY

SIR DAVID BREWSTER, K.H., D.C.L.,

F.R.S., V.P.R.S. EDIN., AND ASSOCIATE OF THE INSTITUTE OF FRANCE.

"Bright star of eve, that send'st thy softening ray
Through the dim twilight of this nether sky,
I hail thy beam like rising of the day,
Hast thou a home for me when I shall die?

"Is there a spot within thy radiant sphere,
Where love, and faith, and truth, again may dwell;
Where I may seek the rest I find not here,
And clasp the cherished forms I loved so well?"

LONDON:

JOHN MURRAY, ALBEMARLE STREET.

1854.

CONTENTS.

PREFACE.

Having been requested by the Editor of the *North British Review* to give an account of a work entitled *Of a Plurality of Worlds, an Essay*, I undertook the task, in the belief that it contained sentiments similar to my own, and that I should have the gratification of illustrating and recommending a doctrine which had long been the creed of the Philosopher, and the hope of the Christian. I was surprised, however, to find that, under a title calculated to mislead the public, the author had made an elaborate attack upon opinions consecrated, as I had thought, by

Reason and Revelation ; and had, in concluding his argument, not only adopted the *Nebular Theory*, so universally condemned as a dangerous speculation, but had taken a view of the condition of the Solar System, calculated to disparage the science of Astronomy, and to throw a doubt over the noblest of its truths.

Under ordinary circumstances I should have contented myself with such an analysis and criticism of the work as could be given within the narrow limits of a Review ; but while the boldness of the author's speculations, and the ingenuity with which they were maintained, required a more elaborate examination of them, the new views which presented themselves to me during the study of the subject, demanded a copious detail of facts which could be given only in a separate Treatise. I have, therefore, devoted the principal part of the volume to a statement of the arguments in favour of a Plurality of Worlds, and have endeavoured, in the subsequent chapters, to answer the various objections urged against it by the author of the Essay, and to examine the grounds upon which he has attempted to establish the extraordinary doctrine, "that the Earth is really the largest planetary body in the Solar System,—its domestic hearth, and the only world in the Universe!"

ST. LEONARD'S COLLEGE, ST. ANDREWS,
April 25th, 1854.

MORE WORLDS THAN ONE.

INTRODUCTION.

THERE is no subject within the whole range of knowledge so universally interesting as that of a Plurality of Worlds. It commands the sympathies, and appeals to the judgment of men of all nations, of all creeds, and of all times; and no sooner do we comprehend the few simple facts on which it rests, than the mind rushes instinctively to embrace it. Before the great truths of Astronomy were demonstrated—before the dimensions and motions of the planets were ascertained, and the fixed stars placed at inconceivable distances from the system to which we belong, philosophers and poets descried in the celestial spheres the abodes of the blest; but it was not till the form and size and motions of the earth were known, and till the condition of the other planets was found to be the same, that analogy compelled us to believe that these planets must be inhabited like our own.

Although this opinion was maintained incidentally by various writers both on astronomy and natural religion, yet M. Fontenelle, Secretary to the Academy of Sciences in Paris, was the first individual who wrote a work expressly on the subject. It was published in 1686, the year before Sir Isaac Newton gave his immortal work, the *Principia*, to the world. It was entitled *Conversations on the Plurality of Worlds*, and consisted of five chapters with the following titles.

1. The Earth is a planet which turns round its own axis and also round the sun.

2. The Moon is a habitable world.

3. Particulars concerning the world in the Moon, and that the other planets are also inhabited.

4. Particulars of the worlds of Venus, Mercury, Mars, Jupiter, and Saturn.

5. The Fixed Stars are as many Suns, each of which illuminates a world.

In another edition of the work published in 1719, Fontenelle added a sixth chapter, entitled, 6. New thoughts which confirm those in the preceding conversations. The latest discoveries which have been made in the heavens.

This singular work, written by a man of great genius, and with a sufficient knowledge of astronomy, excited a high degree of interest, both from the nature of the subject and the vivacity and humour with which it is written. The conversations are carried on with the Marchioness of G——, with whom the author is supposed to be residing. The lady is, of course, distinguished by youth, beauty, and talent, and the share which she takes in the dialogue is not less interesting than the more scientific part assumed by the philosopher.

The *Plurality of Worlds*, as the work was called, was read with unexampled avidity, and was speedily circulated through every part of Europe. It was translated into all the languages of the Continent, and was honoured by annotations from the pen of the celebrated astronomer La Lande, and of M. Gottsched, one of its German editors. No fewer than *three* English translations of it were published, and one of these, we believe the first, had run through *six* editions so early as the year 1737. Wherever it was read it was admired, and though *one hundred and sixty-seven years* have elapsed since its publication, we have not been able to learn that any attempt has been made, during that long period, either to ridicule or controvert the fascinating doctrines which it taught.

A few years after the publication of Fontenelle's work, the celebrated philosopher Christian Huygens, the contemporary of Newton, and the discoverer of the ring and the satellites of Saturn, composed a work on the Plurality of Worlds, under the title of the *Theory of the Universe, or Conjectures concerning the Celestial Bodies and their Inhabitants.*[1] This interesting treatise, as large as that of Fontenelle, has never been translated into English. It was written at the age of sixty-seven, a short time before the author's death, and so great was the interest which he felt in its publication, that he earnestly besought his brother to carry his wishes into effect. He

[1] *Cosmotheoros* sive de Terris Celestibus, earumque ornatu conjecturæ, ad Constantinum Hugenium Fratrem, Gulielmo iii. Magnæ Britanniæ Regi a Secretis. Hugenii *Opera,* tom. ii. pp. 645-722.

mentions the great pleasure he had derived from the composition of it, and from the communication of his views to his friends. About to enter the world of the future, the philosopher who had added new planets to our system, and discovered the most magnificent and incomprehensible of its bodies, looked forward with interest to a solution of the mysteries which it had been the business and the happiness of his life to contemplate. He was anxious that his fellow-men should derive the same pleasure from viewing the planets as the seat of intellectual life, and he left them his Theory of the Universe—a legacy worthy of his name.

The *Cosmotheoros* is a work essentially different from that of Fontenelle. It is didactic and dispassionate, deducing by analogical reasoning a variety of views respecting the plants and animals in the planets, and the general nature and condition of their inhabitants. The work is to some extent a popular Treatise on Astronomy, and contains all that was at that time known respecting the primary and secondary planets of the solar system.

We are not acquainted with any other work

written expressly on the subject of a Plurality of Worlds, but the doctrine was maintained by almost all the distinguished astronomers and writers who have flourished since the true figure of the earth was determined. Giordano Bruno of Nola,[1] Kepler and Tycho believed in it; and Cardinal Cusa and Bruno, before the discovery of binary systems among the stars, believed also that the stars were inhabited. In more modern times Dr. Bentley, Master of Trinity College, Cambridge, in his eighth sermon on the Confutation of Atheism from the origin and frame of the world,[2] has maintained the same doctrine, and in our own day we may number among its supporters the distinguished names of Sir William and Sir John Herschel, Dr. Chalmers, Isaac Taylor, and M. Arago.

Under these circumstances the scientific world has been greatly surprised at the appearance of a work entitled *Of the Plurality of Worlds*, the object of which is to prove that our earth is the only inhabited world in the universe, while its direct tendency is to ridicule and bring into

[1] In his work entitled *Universo e Mondi innumerabili.*

[2] This sermon was written from the information given him by Sir Isaac Newton in his four celebrated letters addressed to Dr. Bentley.

contempt the grand discoveries in sidereal astronomy by which the last century has been distinguished. Although it is not probable that a work of this kind, however ably it is written, and however ingenious may be the reasoning by which views so novel and extraordinary are defended, will influence opinions long and deeply cherished, we have thought it necessary, in defence of astronomical truth, as well as of the lessons which it teaches, to defend the doctrine of a Plurality of Worlds by the aid of modern discoveries, and to analyze and refute the objections which have been made to it in the very remarkable work to which we have referred.

CHAPTER I.

RELIGIOUS ASPECT OF THE QUESTION.

BEFORE Christianity shed its light upon the world, the philosopher who had no other guide but reason, looked beyond the grave for a resting-place from his labours, as well as for a solution of the mysteries which perplexed him. Minds, too, of an inferior order, destined for immortality, and conscious of their destination, instinctively pried into the future, cherishing visions of another world with all the interests of domestic affection, and with all the curiosity which the study of nature inspires. Interesting as has been the past history of our race,—engrossing as must ever be the present,—the future, more exciting still, mingles itself with every thought and sentiment, and casts its beams of hope, or its shadows of fear, over the stage both of active and contemplative life. In youth we scarcely descry it in the distance. To the stripling and the man it appears and disappears like a variable star, shewing in painful succession its spots of light and of shade. In age it looms gigantic to the eye, full of chastened hope and glorious anticipation ; and at the great transition when the outward eye is dim, the image of the future is the last picture which is effaced from the retina of the mind.

But however universal has been the anticipation of the future, and however powerful its influence over the mind, Reason did not venture to give a form and locality to its conceptions ; and the imagination, even with its loosest reins, failed in the attempt. Before the birth of Astronomy, indeed, when our knowledge of space terminated with the ocean or the mountain range that bounded our view, the philosopher could but place his elysium in the sky ; and even when revelation had unveiled the house of many mansions, the Christian sage could but place his future home in the new heavens and in the new earth of his creed. Thus vaguely shadowed forth, thus seen as through a glass darkly, the future even of the Christian, though a reality to his faith, was but a dream to his reason; and in vain did he inquire what this future was to be in its physical relations,—in what region of space it was to be spent,—what duties and pursuits were to occupy it,—and what intellectual and spiritual gifts were to be its portion. But when Science taught us the past history of our earth, its form, and size, and motions,—when Astronomy surveyed the solar system, and measured its planets, and pronounced the earth to be but a tiny sphere, and to have no place of distinction among its gigantic compeers,—and when the Telescope established new systems of worlds far beyond the boundaries of our own, the future of the sage claimed a place throughout the universe, and inspired him with an interest in worlds, and systems of worlds,—in life without limits, as well as in life without end. On eagles' wings he soared to the zenith, and sped his way to the horizon of space, without reaching its ever-retiring bourne; and in the infinity of worlds, and amid the infinity of life, he descried the home and the companions of the future.

That these views are in accordance with the

demonstrated truths of astronomy, and deducible from them by analogies which guide us in the ordinary business of life, it will be the object of this Essay to shew. But before entering upon the astronomical and geological details which will thus demand our attention, some preliminary observations are necessary to prepare our minds for the unfettered discussion of a subject which is still surrounded with many prejudices.

In advocating a plurality of worlds, we are fortunately in a more favoured position than the geologist, whose researches into the ancient history of the earth stood in apparent opposition to the declarations of Scripture. Neither in the Old nor in the New Testament is there a single expression incompatible with the great truth, that there are other worlds than our own which are the seats of life and intelligence. Many passages of Scripture, on the contrary, are favourable to the doctrine, and there are some, we think, which are inexplicable, without admitting it to be true. The beautiful text,[1]

[1] "When I consider thy heavens, the work of thy fingers, the moon and the stars, which thou hast ordained; what is man, that thou art mindful of him? and the son of man, that thou visitest him?"—PSALM viii. 3, 4.

for example, in which the inspired Psalmist expresses his surprise that the Being who fashioned the heavens, and ordained the moon and the stars, should be mindful of so insignificant a being as man, is, we think, a positive argument for a plurality of worlds. We cannot concur in the idea of Dr. Chalmers, that a person wholly ignorant of the science of astronomy, and, consequently, to whom all the stars and planets are but specks of light in the sky, not more important than the *ignis fatuus* upon a marshy field, could express the surprise and deep emotion of the Hebrew poet. We cannot doubt that inspiration revealed to him the magnitude, the distances, and the final cause of the glorious spheres which fixed his admiration. Two portions of creation are here placed in the strongest contrast,—Man in his comparative insignificance, and the Heavens,—the Moon and the Stars in their absolute grandeur. He whom God made a little lower than the angels, whom He crowned with glory and with honour, and for whose redemption He sent His only Son to suffer and to die, could not, in the Psalmist's estimation, be an object of insignificance, and measured, therefore, by his high estimate of man, his idea of the heavens, the moon, and the stars must have been of the most transcendent kind. Had he been ignorant of astronomy, he never could have given utterance to the sentiment in the text. Man, made after God's image, was a nobler creation than twinkling sparks in the sky, or than the larger and more useful lamp of the moon. The Psalmist must, therefore, have written under the impression either that the planets and stars were worlds without life, or worlds inhabited by rational and immortal beings. If he regarded them as unoccupied, we cannot see any reason for surprise that God should be mindful of His noblest work, because innumerable masses of matter existed in the universe, performing, for no intelligible purpose, their solitary rounds. If they were thus made for the benefit and contemplation of man, unseen by any mortal eye but his, then should the Psalmist have expressed his wonder, not at the littleness, but at the greatness of the being for whose use such magnificent worlds had been called into existence. But if the poet viewed these worlds, as he doubtless did, as teeming with life physical and intellectual, as globes which may have required millions of years for their preparation, exhibiting new forms of being, new powers of mind, new conditions in the past, and new glories in the future, we can then understand why he marvelled at the care of God for creatures so *comparatively* insignificant as man.

It is evident, from the text we have been considering, and from other passages of Scripture, that the word *Heavens*, so distinctly separated from the moon and the stars, represents a material creation, the work of God's fingers, and not a celestial space in which spiritual beings may be supposed to dwell ; and we are therefore entitled to attach the same meaning to the term wherever it occurs, unless the context forbids such an application of it. The writers, both in the Old and New Testament, speak of the heavens as a separate material creation from the earth, and there are passages which seem very clearly to indicate that they are the seat of life. When St. Paul tells us that the *worlds* were framed by the word of God, and that by our Saviour, the heir of all things, He made the *worlds*, we are not entitled to suppose that he means globes of matter, revolving without inhabitants, or without any preparation for receiving them. He can only mean *worlds* like our own, that declare to their living occupants the glory of their Maker. When Isaiah speaks of the heavens being *spread out as a tent to dwell in*,[1] when Job tells us that God, who *spread out the heavens, made Arcturus, Orion and Pleiades*, and the *chambers* of the south,[2] and when Amos speaks of Him who buildeth His stories in the heavens,[3] (His house of *many mansions*,) they use terms which clearly indicate that the celestial spheres are the seat of life. In the book of Genesis, too, God is said to have finished the heavens and the earth, and *all the host of them*.[4] Nehemiah declares that God made the *heaven, the heaven of heavens, and all their host*, the earth and all things that are therein, and that *the host of heaven worship Him*.[5] The Psalmist speaks of *all the host of the heavens as made by the breath of God's mouth*,[6] (the process by

[1] Isaiah xlv. 22. [2] Job ix. 8, 9. [3] Amos ix. 6.
[4] Gen. ii. 1. [5] Neh. ix. 6. [6] Psalm xxxiii. 6.

which He gave life to Adam ;) and Isaiah furnishes us with a striking passage, in which the occupants of the earth and of the heavens are separately described. "I have made the earth, and created man upon it: I, even my hands, have stretched out the heavens, and all *their host have I commanded.*"[1] But in addition to these obvious references to life and things pertaining to life, we find in Isaiah the following remarkable passage, "For thus, saith the Lord, that created the heavens, God himself that formed the earth and made it; he hath established it, *he created it* NOT IN VAIN, *he formed it* TO BE INHABITED."[2] Here we have a distinct declaration from the inspired prophet, that the *earth would have been created* IN VAIN *if it had not been formed to be inhabited;* and hence we draw the conclusion, that as the Creator cannot be supposed to have made the worlds of our system, and those in the sidereal universe in vain, they must have been formed *to be inhabited.*

These views, as deduced from Scripture, receive much support from considerations of a

1 Isaiah xlv. 12. 2 Isaiah xlv. 18.

very different nature. Man in his future state of existence is to consist, as at present, of a spiritual nature residing in a corporeal frame. He must live therefore upon a material planet, subject to all the laws of matter, and performing functions for which a material body is indispensable. We must therefore find, for the race of Adam, if not for races that preceded him, a material home upon which he may reside, or from which he may travel by means unknown to us, to other localities in the universe. That home, we think, cannot be the *new earth* upon which we dwell, though it may be the *new heavens* wherein dwelleth righteousness. At the present hour the population of the earth is nearly *a thousand millions ;* and by whatever process we may compute the numbers that have existed before the present generation, and estimate those that are yet to inherit the earth, we shall obtain a population which the habitable parts of our globe could not possibly accommodate. If there is not room then on our globe for the millions of millions of beings who have lived and died upon its surface, and who may yet live and die during the period fixed for its occupation by man, we can scarcely doubt that their future abode must be on some of the primary or secondary planets of the Solar system, whose inhabitants have ceased to exist like those on the earth, or upon planets which have long been in a state of preparation, as our earth was, for the advent of intellectual life.

The connexion thus indicated between the destinies of the human family and the material system to which we belong, arising from the limited extent of the earth's habitable surface, and its unlimited population, is a strong corroboration of the views which we have deduced from Scripture. In the world of instinct the superabundance of life is controlled by the law of mutual destruction, which reigns in the earth, the ocean, and the air; but the swarm of human life, increasing in an incalculable ratio, both in the Old and the New World, has not been perceptibly reduced by the scythe of famine, of pestilence, or of war; and when we consider the length of time during which this accumulation may proceed, we cannot justly challenge the correctness of the conclusion that this earth is not to be the future residence of the numerous family which it has reared. The connexion between this probable truth and the doctrine of a plurality of worlds, will appear from the facts and reasonings in the following chapter.

CHAPTER II.

DESCRIPTION OF THE SOLAR SYSTEM.

In order to appreciate the force of the argument for a plurality of worlds, derived from the similarity of our earth to the other planets of the Solar system, we must call the attention of the reader to a popular description of the magnitudes, distances, and general phenomena of the different bodies that compose it.

In making this survey, the first and the grandest object which arrests our attention is the glorious Sun,—the centre and soul of our system,—the lamp that lights it, the fire that heats it,—the magnet that guides and controls it,—the fountain of colour which gives its azure to the sky, its verdure to the fields, its rainbow hues to the gay world of flowers, and the "purple light of love" to the marble cheek of youth and beauty. This globe, probably of burning gas, enveloping a solid nucleus, is nearly 900,000 miles in diameter, above a hundred times the diameter of our globe, and five hundred times larger in bulk than all the planets put together! It revolves upon its axis in twenty-five days, and throws off its light with the velocity of 192,000 miles in a second. Sometimes by the naked eye, but frequently even by small telescopes, large black spots, many thousand miles in diameter, are seen upon its surface, and are evidently openings in the luminous atmosphere, through which we see the opaque solid nucleus, or the real body of the sun.

Around, and nearest the sun, at a distance of thirty-six millions of miles, revolves the planet MERCURY, with a day of twenty-four hours, and a year of eighty-eight days; and he receives from the sun nearly seven times as much light and heat as the earth. Through the telescope some astronomers have observed spots on its surface, and mountains several miles in height.

Next to Mercury the planet VENUS revolves at the distance of sixty-eight millions of miles, with a day of nearly twenty-four hours, and a year of 224 days. Her diameter is 7700 miles, a little less than that of the earth. She changes her phases like the moon, exhibits spots on her surface, and, according to Schroeter, has mountains nearly twenty miles in height. The light and heat which she receives from the sun is about double of that which is received by the earth.[1]

The next body of the Solar system is our own Earth—our birthplace, and soon to be our grave. Its distance from the sun is ninety-six millions of miles ; its diameter nearly 8000 ; its year 365 days, and its day twenty-four hours. The form of the Earth is that of an oblate spheroid, or of a sphere flattened at the poles like an orange. Its superficies is divided into continents and seas, the continents occupying *one-third*, and the seas *two-thirds* of its whole surface. The land, sometimes level and sometimes undulating, occasionally rises into groups and ranges of mountains, the highest of which does not exceed five miles. The Earth is sur-

[1] From the rare appearance and want of permanence in the spots of Mercury and Venus, Sir John Herschel is of opinion, " that we do not see as in the moon the real surface of these planets, but only their atmospheres, much loaded with clouds, and which may serve to mitigate the otherwise intense glare of their sunshine."—*Outlines of Astronomy*, § 509.

rounded with an aerial envelope or atmosphere, which is computed to be about forty-five miles in height, though the region of clouds does not reach much above the summits of the highest mountains.

The Earth is accompanied by a MOON or satellite, whose distance is 237,000 miles, and diameter 2160. Her surface is composed of hill and dale, of rocks and mountains nearly two miles high, and of circular cavities, sometimes five miles in depth, and forty in diameter, which are believed to be the remains of extinct volcanoes. She possesses neither *lakes* nor *seas*; and we cannot discover with the telescope any traces of living beings, or any monuments of their hands, though we hope it will be done with some magnificent telescope which may yet be constructed. Viewing the Earth as the *third* planet in order from the sun, can we doubt that it is a globe like the rest, poised in ether like them, and, like them, moving round the central luminary?

Next, beyond the Earth, is the red-coloured planet MARS, with a day of about twenty-five hours, and revolving round the sun in 687 days.

at the distance of one hundred and forty-two millions of miles. His diameter is 4100 miles, and his surface exhibits spots of different hues, —the seas, according to Sir John Herschel, being *green*, and the land *red*. The spots which have been seen on this planet by several astronomers, are not always equally distinct, but when seen "they offer," as Sir John Herschel observes, "the appearance of forms, considerably definite and highly characteristic, brought successively into view by the rotation of the planet, from the assiduous observation of which it has even been found practicable to construct a rude chart of the surface of the planet. The variety in the spots may arise from the planet not being destitute of atmosphere and cloud ; and what adds greatly to the probability of this, is the appearance of brilliant white spots at its poles, which have been conjectured, with some probability, to be snow, as they disappear when they have been long exposed to the sun, and are greatest when just emerging from the long night of their polar winter, the snow line then extending to about six degrees from the pole."[1]

[1] *Outlines of Astronomy*, § 510.

Hitherto we have been surveying worlds at a respectful distance from each other, and having days, and nights, and seasons, and aspects, of the same character; but we now arrive at a region in space where some great catastrophe has doubtless taken place. At the distance of about two hundred and fifty millions of miles from the sun, corresponding to a period of about 1500 days, astronomers long ago predicted the existence of a large planet, occupying the space between Mars and Jupiter. In the beginning of the present century, one very small planet was discovered in this locality by M. Piazzi; and after other two had been discovered, one by himself, Dr. Olbers hazarded the opinion that the *three* planets were fragments of a larger one which had burst; and this remarkable theory has been almost placed beyond a doubt by the discovery, in the same place, of *twenty-nine* fragments in all, chiefly by M. Gasparis of Naples, and our own countryman, Mr. Hind.

Beyond this remarkable group is situated the planet JUPITER, a world of huge magnitude, revolving round its axis in ten hours, and round the sun in 4333 days, (a little less than twelve years,) at the distance of four hundred and eighty-five millions of miles. His form is that of an oblate spheroid, his equatorial being to his polar diameter as 107 to 100. His diameter is 90,000 miles, and he is attended by *four* satellites, the average size of which is a little greater than that of our moon. His surface exhibits bright spots and dark bands or belts, which, though they have always the same direction, vary in breadth and in position, occasionally running into branches and dark spots. Sir John Herschel is of opinion, that the belts are tracts of corresponding clear sky in the planet's atmosphere, through which the darker body of the planet is seen, and that they are produced by currents like our trade-winds, but having a more steady and decided character.

Next to Jupiter is the remarkable planet SATURN, accompanied with *eight* satellites, and surrounded by a *ring*, separated from his body by an interval of 19,000 miles. The distance of Saturn from the sun is eight hundred and ninety millions of miles, his annual period twenty-nine and a half years, and the length of his day ten and a half hours. His diameter is 76,000 miles, and the outer diameter of his ring 176,000. According to very recent observations, the ring is divided into *three* separate rings, which, according to the calculations of Mr. Bond, an American astronomer, must be fluid. He is of opinion that the number of rings is continually changing, and that their maximum number, in the normal condition of the mass, does not exceed *twenty*. According to Mr. Bond, the power which sustains the centre of gravity of the *ring* is not in the planet itself, but in his satellites; and the satellites, though constantly disturbing the ring, actually sustain it in the very act of perturbation.

Mr. Otto Struve and Mr. Bond have lately studied, with the great Munich telescope, at the observatory of Pulkowa, the *third* ring of Saturn, which Mr. Lassels and Mr. Bond discovered to be *fluid*. They saw distinctly the dark interval between this fluid ring and the two old ones, and even measured its dimensions; and they perceived at its inner margin an edge feebly illuminated, which they thought might be the commencement of a fourth ring. These astronomers are of opinion, that the fluid ring is not of very recent formation, and that it is not subject to rapid change; and they have come to the extraordinary conclusion, that the inner border of the ring has, since the time of Huygens, been gradually approaching to the body of Saturn, and that *we may expect sooner or later, perhaps in some dozen of years, to see the rings united with the body of the planet.*

Beyond Saturn, at a distance from the sun of one thousand eight hundred millions of miles, is placed the planet URANUS, discovered by Dr. Herschel. Its year, or annual period, is eighty-four years, and the length of its day nine and a half hours. Its diameter is 34,500 miles, and it is attended by *eight* satellites, six of which were discovered by Dr. Herschel, and the other two, a few years ago, by Mr. Lassels of Liverpool.

The remotest planet of our system, the planet NEPTUNE, discovered theoretically in 1846 by Adams and Leverrier, and first recognised in the heavens by M. Galle of Berlin, is about 42,000 miles in diameter, and performs its annual revolution in 63,000 days, (about 145 years,) at the distance of nearly *three thousand millions* of miles from the sun. It is accompanied with one, and probably two, satellites; and there is reason to believe that it is surrounded with a ring like Saturn.

Having thus travelled from the centre to the verge of the planetary system,—from the effulgent orb of day to that almost cimmerian twilight where Phœbus could scarcely see to guide his steeds, let us ponder a while over the startling yet instructive sights which we have encountered in our course. Adjoining the sun, we find Mercury and Venus, with days and seasons like ours. Upon reaching our own planet, we recognise in it the same general features, but we find it larger in magnitude, and possessing the additional distinction of a satellite and a race of living beings to rejoice in the pre-eminence. In contrast with Mars, our earth still maintains its superiority both in size and equipments; but, upon advancing a little farther into space, our pride is rebuked and our fears evoked, when we reach the part of our system where *twenty-nine* asteroids, relics of a once mighty planet, (or the uncombined portions of what might have been a planet,) are revolving in dissevered orbits, and warning the vain astronomer of another world that a similar fate may await his own. Dejected, but not despairing, we pass onward, and, as if in bright contrast with the confusion and desolation we have witnessed, there bursts upon our sight the splendid orb of Jupiter, proudly enthroned amid his attendant satellites. When compared with so glorious a creation, our own earth dwindles into insignificance. It is no longer the monarch of the planetary throng, and we blush at the recollection that sovereigns and pontiffs, and even philosophers, made it the central ball, around which the Sun and Moon and planets, and even the stars, revolved in obsequious subjection. The dignity of being the seat of intellectual and animal life, however, still seems to be our own; and if our globe does not swell so largely to the eye, or shine so brightly in the night, it has yet been the seat of glorious dynasties,—of mighty empires,—of heroes that have bled for their country,—of martyrs who have died for their faith,—and of sages who have unravelled the very universe we are surveying. Pursuing our outward course, a new wonder is presented to us in the gorgeous appendages of Saturn, encircled with a brilliant ring, and with eight moons, for the use, doubtless, of living beings. Advancing onwards, we encounter Uranus, with his eight pledges that he is the seat of life ; and after passing the new planet Neptune, at the frontier of our system, we reach what is the region, and what may be regarded as the home, of comets.

COMETS, or wandering stars, as they have been called, are those celestial bodies most of which appear occasionally only within the limits of the Solar system. They move in elliptical orbits, in one of the foci of which the sun is placed ; but, unlike the planets, which always move from west to east, the comets revolve in orbits inclined at all possible angles, and move in all possible directions. The movements of the six or seven hundred comets which have been observed, must be chiefly executed within that vast and untenanted region, which lies between the nearest known fixed star and the orbit of *Neptune*, an interval equal to six thousand times the distance of that planet from the sun, or twenty-one million million of miles. What is their occupation there, or what it is here, when they are our visitors, we cannot venture to guess. That they do not perform the functions of planets is obvious, from their very nature; and there is no appearance of their importing anything useful into our system, or of their exporting anything to another. Judging from the immense portion of their orbits which lies beyond Neptune, it has been imagined that the central body of some other system is placed in the distant focus of each of their orbits, and that in this way all the different systems in the universe are, as it were, united into one by the intercommunication of comets. Some comets have passed near the earth, and others may pass still nearer it; but even if they should not produce those tremendous effects which Laplace has indicated, and if their great rarity and rapid motion should hinder them from acting upon our seas, or changing the axis of our globe, a sweep of their train of gas or of vapour would not be a pleasing salutation to living beings. The greatest distance of the most distant comet that has been observed, falls short of the distance of the nearest fixed star by *nine million million of miles.* Placing ourselves at this distance, how ridiculous appears the idea, so long and devoutly cherished, that the heavens, with all their host, revolved round our little planet! At that point the earth is not even visible, and the whole starry creation, and our sun itself dwindled into a star, stand fixed and immovable.

Till within the last forty years it was the universal belief among astronomers that every comet strayed far beyond the limits of the Solar system, the shortest period of any of those that had been observed being about *seventy* years, indicating the immense distance which it must have traversed beyond the orbit of Neptune. In 1818, however, M. Pons discovered a comet, now called *Encke's Comet*, whose period was not above *three years* and five months, and whose orbit, extending inwards as far as that of Mercury, did not reach beyond the orbit of Pallas. Other *five* comets, whose periods are $5\frac{1}{2}$, $5\frac{4}{7}$, $6\frac{3}{4}$, $7\frac{1}{2}$, and sixteen years, have been discovered within the limits of our system. Among these bodies, the *comet of Biela*, discovered in 1826, appeared to separate *into two distinct comets* with parallel tails, which after a certain time resumed its single state. M. Damoiseau having predicted that this comet would pass within 18,000 miles of a point in the earth's orbit, the publication of this fact excited such an alarm in Paris, that M. Arago was summoned from his studies to allay the terror of the community. The fears of the people, however, will not appear unreasonable, when we recollect that Sir John Herschel has stated that the orbit of this comet "so nearly intersects that of the earth, that an actual collision is not impossible, and indeed must in all likelihood happen in the lapse of some millions of years!"

A seventh comet belonging to our system, called *Lexell's Comet*, which that astronomer discovered in 1770, is supposed *to have been lost*, as it ought to have appeared *thirteen* times, and has not been seen since that date. It is supposed to have been rendered invisible in 1779 by the action of Jupiter, but in what way astronomers have not been able to determine.

The following popular view of the sizes and

distances of the planets which compose the Solar system has been given by Sir John Herschel:

	Size.	Diameter of orbit in feet.
The Sun, .	a Globe two feet in diameter, .	0
Mercury, . .	a Mustard Seed, . . .	164
Venus, . .	a Pea, ...	284
Earth, . .	a larger Pea, . . .	430
Mars, . .	a large Pin's head, . .	654
Juno, Ceres, Vesta, Pallas, and the other 25 Asteroids,	Grains of Sand, ...	1000 to 1200
Jupiter, . .	an Orange, . .	Half a mile.
Saturn, . .	a Small Orange, .	One mile and a fifth.
Uranus, . .	a Cherry, . .	A mile and a half.
Neptune, .	a Plum, . .	Two miles and a half.

To which we may add,

The greatest distance of a Comet,	Eight thousand miles.
Distance of nearest Fixed Star,	Fifteen thousand miles.

CHAPTER III.

THE GEOLOGICAL CONDITION OF THE EARTH.

In the preceding brief description of the Solar system, we see distinctly the relation which our own Earth bears to the other planets, in its position, its form, its magnitude, its satellite, and its daily and annual motions. But though a comparison of these properties of the earth, which constitute what may be called its *astronomical condition*, with the analogous properties of the other planets, might entitle us to ascribe to them other functions,—the function, for example, of supporting inhabitants, which the earth only is known to possess, yet our argument will derive new strength, and we shall be prepared to meet recent objections, by taking into consideration the geological structure of the earth, and the properties of its atmosphere, and by endeavouring to read its past history in the successive steps by which it has been prepared as a residence for the human family.

The earth, as we have seen, when merely examined by the eye, consists of land and water. The land is composed of soils of various kinds, and of stones and rocks of different characters. It is formed into extensive plains, into valleys excavated apparently by rivers or water-courses, and into mountain groups and mountain ranges, rising to the height of several miles above the bed of the ocean. In order to obtain a knowledge of the structure of the earth, geologists have examined with the greatest care its soils and its rocks, wherever they have been laid bare by natural or artificial causes, by the operation of the miner, or the road engineer, or by the action of rivers or of the sea; and they have thus obtained certain general results which give us an approximate idea of the different materials which compose what is called the *crust of the earth.* In those portions of its surface, which do not rise into mountains, the thickness of the crust thus explored does not exceed *ten miles*, which is only the 800th part of the earth's diameter,—a quantity so small, that if we represent the earth by a sphere having the same diameter as the cupola of St. Paul's, which is 140 feet, the thickness of the crust would be only about *two inches.*

Beneath the crust lies the *Nucleus* of the earth, or its *kernel* or its *skeleton* frame, of the nature and composition of which we are entirely ignorant. We know only, by comparing the average density of the earth, which is about 5½ times that of water, with the average density of the rocks near its surface, which is about 2½ times that of water, that the density of the nucleus, if of uniform solidity, must exceed 5½, and must be much greater if it is hollow or contains large cavities. Geology does not pretend to give us any information respecting the process by which the nucleus of the earth was formed. Some speculative astronomers indeed have presumptuously embarked in such an inquiry; but there is not a trace of evidence that the solid nucleus of the globe was formed by secondary causes, such as the aggregation of attenuated matter diffused through space; and the *nebular theory*, as it has been called, though maintained by a few distinguished names, has, we think, been overturned by arguments that have never been answered. Sir Isaac Newton, in his four celebrated letters to Dr. Bentley, has demonstrated that the planets of the solar system could not have been thus formed, and put in motion round a central sun.

But though geologists have not been able to give us any intelligence respecting the earth's nucleus, they have examined the rocks which rest upon it, or the lowest of the series which extend upwards to the surface of the earth.

I. The lowest of these rocks are granite, granitic rocks, trap, and porphyry. They are composed chiefly of the simple minerals, *Quartz*, *Feldspar*, *Mica*, and *Hornblende*. They are consequently crystalline and unstratified, and are believed to be of igneous origin.

The next series of rocks are what are called the *Metamorphic or altered rocks*. They consist of gneiss, mica slate, and clay slate, and are more or less stratified.

The next series of rocks is Basalt, or ancient lava, and what are called Trachytic Rocks.

To these rocks the name of *Primary* has

been given, and also the appellation of *Azoic*, because they contain no traces of plants or animals, and are therefore *without life*, or destitute of organic remains.

Above these formations lie the *Secondary* and the *Tertiary* formations.

II. The *Secondary* formations have been divided by Professor Ansted into *three* periods, the *Older*, the *Middle*, and the *Newer* Secondary.

1. The *Older Secondary* formation he again divides into the *Older Palæozoic* period, namely, 1. The *Lower Silurian* rocks, to which the name of *Protozoic* has been given, because they contain the *first* traces of *life;* and, 2. The *Upper Silurian* rocks, the *Middle Palæozoic* period, containing the Devonian or Old Red Sandstone formation; and

The *Newer* Palæozoic period, including, 1. The *Carboniferous* formation; and, 2. The *Magnesian Limestone*, or Permian formation, and above these strata lie—

The *Upper New Red Sandstone* or Triassic formation, the last member of the older secondary period.

2. The *Middle secondary* formation, consists of the *Lias*, *Oolite*, and *Wealden* formations; and,

3. The *Newer secondary* period consists of the *Cretaceous* or chalk formation.

III. The *Tertiary formation* consists, reckoning from below, of,—

1. The *older tertiary*, or *Eocene*, viz., Bagshot sand and London clay.
2. The *middle tertiary*, or *Miocene*, viz., Red and Coralline Rag.
3. The *newer tertiary*, or *Pliocene*, viz., the Till of Clyde and Norwich Crag.
4. The *superficial deposits*, or *Pleistocene*, viz., all diluvial and alluvial deposits of gravel and other materials, sometimes stratified.

The proportional thicknesses of these different formations have been estimated by Professor

Phillips as follows, but the numbers can be regarded only as a very rude estimate :—

Tertiary formation,	2,000	feet.
Cretaceous,	1,100	,,
Oolite and Lias,	2,500	,,
New Red Sandstone,	2,000	,,
Carboniferous,	10,000	,,
Old Red Sandstone,	9,000	,,
Primitive Rocks,	20,000	,,
Thickness of the Earth's crust,	46,600 = 9 miles nearly.	

As all the stratified formations which compose the crust of the earth have obviously been deposited in succession, geologists have endeavoured to form some notion of the time occupied in their deposition, or the age of the most ancient of them. By studying the fossil remains found in the different formations, geologists have placed it beyond a doubt, that great changes have taken place during the formation of the crust of the earth. The plants and animals which existed in one period are not found in another,—new species were at different times created,—and frequent convulsions have taken place, upheaving the beds of the ocean into continents and mountain ranges, and covering the dry land with the waters which were displaced. That the deposition of strata of such thickness, and operations of such magnitude, required a long period of time for their accomplishment, has been willingly conceded to the geologist; but this concession has been founded on the adoption of a *unit* of measure which may or may not be correct. It is taken for granted, that many of the stratified rocks were deposited in the sea by the *same slow processes* which are going on in the present day; and as the thickness of the deposits now produced is a very small quantity during a long period of time, it is inferred that *nine* or *ten miles of strata* must have taken millions of years for their formation.

We are not disposed to grudge the geologist even periods so marvellous as this, provided they are considered as merely hypothetical; but when we find, as we shall presently do, that speculative writers employ these assumed periods as positive truths, for establishing other theories which we consider erroneous, and even dangerous, we are compelled to examine more minutely a chronology which has been thus misapplied.

Although we may admit that our seas and continents have nearly the same locality, and cover nearly the same area as they did at the creation of Adam; and that the hills have not since that time changed their form or their height; nor the beds of the ocean become deeper or shallower from the diurnal changes going on around us,—yet this does not authorize us to conclude that the world was prepared for man by similar causes operating in a similar manner. The same physical causes may operate quickly or slowly. The dew may fall invisibly on the ground,—the gentle shower may descend noiseless on the grass,—or the watery vapour may rush down in showers and torrents of rain, destroying animal and vegetable life. The frozen moisture may fall in atoms of crystal, which are felt only by the tender skin upon which they light; or it may come down in flakes of snow, forming beds many feet in thickness; or it may be precipitated in destructive hailstones, or in masses of ice which crush everything upon which they fall.

When the earth was completed as the home of the human family, violent changes upon its surface were incompatible with the security of life, and the progress of civilisation. The powers of the physical world were therefore put under restraint, when man obtained dominion over the earth; and after the great catastrophe which destroyed almost every living thing, the "bow was set in the clouds," a covenant, between God and man, that the elements should not again be his destroyer. If the Almighty then, since the creation of man, "broke up the fountains of the deep, and opened the windows of the heavens," and thus, by apparently natural causes, covered the whole earth with an ocean that rose above the Himalaya and the Andes,—why may He not at different periods, or during the whole course of the earth's formation, have deposited its strata by a rapid precipitation of their atoms from the waters which suspended them? The period of the earth's formation would, upon this principle, be reduced to little more than the united generations of the different orders of plants and animals which constitute its organic remains. But even the period thus computed from the supposed duration of animal life may be still farther shortened. Plants and animals which, in our day, require a century for their development, may in primitive times have shot up in rank luxuriance, and been ready, in a few days, or months, or years, for the great purpose of exhibiting, by their geological distribution, the progressive formation of the earth.

There are other points, in geological theory, which, though mere inferences from a very limited number of facts, have been employed, as if they were absolutely true, to support erroneous and dangerous theories; and but for this misapplication of them we should not have called in question opinions in themselves reasonable only when viewed as probable truths. The geological inference to which we allude is, that man did not exist during the period of the earth's formation. No work of human skill—no fragment of the skeleton—no remains of the integuments of man have been found among the plants and animals which occupy the graves of primæval times. If it be quite certain, or rather sufficiently credible, which we think it is, that all the formations with fossil remains were deposited before the advent of Adam, it is barely possible that pre-adamite races may have inhabited the earth simultaneously with the animals which characterize its different formations. But though possible, and to a certain extent available, as the basis of an argument against a startling theory, we cannot admit its probability. Man, as now constituted, could not have lived amid the storms and earthquakes and eruptions of a world in the act of formation. His timid nature would have quailed under the multifarious convulsions around him. The thunder of a boiling and tempest-driven ocean would have roused him from his couch, as its waters rushed upon him at midnight: Torrents of lava or of mud would have chased him from his hearth; and if he escaped the pestilence from animal and vegetable death, the vapour of the subterranean alembics would have suffocated him in the open air. The house of the child of civilisation was not ready for his reception. The stones that were to build and roof it, had not quitted their native beds. The coal that was to light and heat it, was either green in the forest, or blackening in the storehouse of the deep. The iron that was to defend him from external violence, lay buried in the ground; and the rich materials of civilisation, the gold, the silver, and the gems, even if they were ready, had not been cast within his reach, from the hollow of the Creator's hand.

But if man could have existed amid catastrophes so tremendous and privations so severe, his presence was not required, for his intellectual powers could have had no suitable employment. Creation was the field on which his industry was to be exercised and his genius unfolded; and that Divine reason which was to analyze and combine, would have sunk into sloth before the elements of matter were let loose from their prison-house, and Nature had cast them in her mould. But though there was no specific time in this vast chronology which we could fix as appropriate for the appearance of man, yet we now perceive that he entered with dignity at its close. When the sea was gathered into one place, and the dry land appeared, a secure footing was provided for our race. When the waters above the firmament were separated from the waters below it, and when the light which ruled the day, and the light which ruled the night, were displayed in the azure sky, man could look upward into the infinite of space, as he looked downward into the infinite in time. When the living creature after his kind appeared in the fields, and the seed-bearing herb covered the earth, human genius was enabled to estimate the power, and wisdom, and bounty of its Author, and human labour received and accepted its commission, when it was declared from on high that seed-time and harvest should never cease upon the earth.

But though we think it probable from these considerations, that intellectual races could not occupy the earth during its formation, yet we know not what disclosures might be made had we the power of examining the whole of the strata which girdle the earth. The dry land upon our globe occupies only *one-fourth* of its whole superficies—all the rest is sea. How much of this *fourth* part have geologists been able to examine? and how small seems to be the area of stratification which has been explored? We venture to say not *one-fiftieth* part of the whole, and yet upon the results of so partial a survey, there has been founded a startling generalization. The intellectual races, if they did exist, must have lived at a distance from the ferocious animals that may have occupied the seas and the jungles of the ancient world, and consequently their remains could not have been found in the ordinary fossiliferous strata. Their dwelling-place may have been in one or more of the numerous localities of our continents not yet explored, or in those immense regions of the earth which are now covered by the great oceans of the globe ; and till these oceans have quitted their beds, or some great convulsions have upheaved and laid bare the strata above which the races in question may have lived and died, we are not entitled to maintain it as a demonstrated truth, that the ancient earth was under the sole dominion of the brutes that perish.

But without waiting for the result of catastrophes like these, the future of geology, even if restricted to existing continents and islands, may be pregnant with startling discoveries, and the remains of intellectual races may be found even beneath the primitive *Azoic* formations of the earth. The astronomers of the present day have penetrated far into the celestial depths, compared with those of the preceding age,—descrying in the remotest space glorious creations, and establishing mighty laws. Like them, may not geologists descend deeper into the abyss beneath, and discover in caverns yet unexplored the upheaved cemeteries of primordial times. The earth has yet to surrender its strongholds of gigantic secrets,—and startling revelations are yet to be read on sepulchres of stone. It is not from that distant bourne where the last ray of starlight trembles on the telescopic eye that man is to receive the great secret of the world's birth, or of his future destiny. It is from the deep vaults to which primæval life has been consigned that the history of the dawn of life is to be composed. Geologists have read that chronology backwards, and are decyphering downwards its pale and perishing alphabet. They have reached the embryos of vegetable existence, the probable terminus of the formation which has buried them. But who can tell *what sleeps beyond!* Another creation may lie beneath—more glorious creatures may be entombed there. The mortal coils of beings more lovely, more pure, more divine than man, may yet read to us the unexpected lesson that we have not been the first, and may not be the last of the intellectual race.

In order to compare the condition of the earth with that of the moon and the other planets of the Solar system, we must know something of its atmosphere, of its action in refracting, reflecting, and polarizing light, and of the phenomena which it will exhibit to other planets in its various states, as modified by the aqueous vapour which it contains, whether it exists in minute vesicles, or in masses of clouds. The light reflected by the atmosphere, when in its purest state, is a *rich blue*, becoming paler and paler as the aqueous vapour is increased. When the light of the sun reaches the eye, after having been transmitted through great lengths of the earth's atmosphere, it is bright *red*, passing into *orange* and *yellow* when the length of its path is diminished. Considering, then, the diversity of climate in any one hemisphere of the globe, it is hardly possible that the earth, as seen from any given point in space, could appear free from clouds. When the sky is blue over large portions of the tropical regions, and smaller portions of the temperate and arctic zones, it is elsewhere covered with fleecy clouds, or throwing down its superabundant vapours in rain, or hail, or snow. The banks of fleecy clouds will reflect a brilliant light to the distant eye, while the pure air will exhibit the colour of the land, or of the ocean, mixed with its own native tint of blue; and, in certain positions of the sun, the red beams into which his pure rays have been changed by absorption, will display themselves in certain parts of the terrestrial disc. When the Earth, therefore, is reduced by distance to the apparent size of Mars and Jupiter, it will exhibit a tint composed of all those which we have described.

When the blue light of the sky, and the reflected light of the clouds, are examined by an observer on the surface of the earth, it is found to be polarized, like the light which is reflected from the surfaces of transparent bodies;[1] and, therefore, a greater or less portion of the light which reaches the eye of an observer, placed on another planet, must be polarized, and exhibit all the properties of that species of light. We thus obtain a certain test of the existence of water in the other planets of the system, and we are enabled to ascertain the truth of certain speculations respecting their condition, which affect the question of a plurality of worlds.

[1] See Johnston's *Physical Atlas*.

CHAPTER IV.

ANALOGY BETWEEN THE EARTH AND THE OTHER PLANETS.

WITH the information contained in the preceding chapter, respecting the structure of the earth and its atmosphere, we are now in a condition to compare it as an inhabited world with the other planets of our system, and to ascertain, from the analogies which exist between them, to what extent it is probable that they are either inhabited, or in a state of preparation, as the earth once was, for the reception of inhabitants.

In making this comparison, the first point which demands our attention is the *position* which the earth occupies in the Solar system. In reference to the number of the planets, which is *nine*, reckoning the asteroids as *one*, Jupiter is the *fifth*, or middle planet, and is otherwise highly distinguished. Our earth, therefore, is neither the *middle* planet nor the planet *nearest* the sun, nor the planet *farthest* from that luminary. In reference to the light and heat which the planets receive from the sun, the Earth has neither the warmest, nor the middle, nor the coldest place. With respect to the number of moons or satellites, the only uses of which that we know, is to give light to the planet, and produce tides in its seas, the Earth has the lowest number, all the planets exterior to it having a larger number. If we compare it with the other planets in reference to their size, their form, their density, the length of their year, the length of their day, the eccentricity of their orbits, we shall find that in all these cases the earth is not in any respect distinguished above the rest. Hence we are entitled to conclude that the Earth, as a planet, has no pre-eminence in the Solar system to induce us to believe that it is the only inhabited world, or has any claim to be peculiarly favoured by the Creator.

In order to shew the high probability that the other planets are either inhabited, or in a state of preparation for the reception of inhabitants, we shall now proceed to compare the Earth with the planet *Jupiter*, one of the planets farther from the sun than ours, and then with *Venus*, one of the planets nearer the sun,—these planets representing the two groups into which the system may be divided.

The diameter of Jupiter being 87,000 miles, and that of the Earth 7926, the relative size or bulk of the two planets will be proportional to the squares of these numbers. Hence the size or bulk of Jupiter is 1200 times greater than that of the Earth, and this alone is a proof that it must have been made for some *grand* and *useful* purpose. Like the Earth it is flattened at its poles, and it revolves round its axis in $9^h\ 56^m$, which is the length of its day. It enjoys different climates, and different seasons in its year; but, what especially demands our attention, it is illuminated by four moons, capable of supplying it with abundance of light during the short absence of the sun. Owing to the small inclination of Jupiter's axis to the plane of its orbit, which is only about *three* degrees, there is so little change in the temperature of its seasons, that it may be said to enjoy a perpetual spring. The rotation of the Earth about its axis produces currents in its atmosphere parallel to the equator, which have received the name of the *trade winds.* On the surface of Jupiter astronomers have observed streaks or belts to the number of thirty, some of which extend to a great distance from its equator. Large spots, which change their form, have also been frequently seen upon Jupiter. M. Madler, by whom these observations have been chiefly made, is of opinion, that owing to the length of Jupiter's year, and the small change which takes place in the seasons, the masses of clouds in his atmosphere have their form, position, and arrangement more permanent than those in the atmosphere of the Earth, and he thinks it probable that the inhabitants in latitudes greater than 40° may never see the firmament.

The satellites of Jupiter afford him perpetual moonlight. They suffer eclipses like our moon when they encounter his huge shadow, and they frequently eclipse the sun when they pass between him and the planet. These satellites afford to their primary planet four months of different lengths, one of which is four Jovian days, and the next *eight*, *seventeen*, and *forty* days respectively.

With so many striking points of resemblance between the Earth and Jupiter, the unprejudiced mind cannot resist the conclusion that Jupiter has been created like the Earth for the express purpose of being the seat of animal and intellectual life. The Atheist and the Infidel, the Christian and the Mahometan,—men of all creeds and nations and tongues,—the philosopher and the unlettered peasant, have all rejoiced in this universal truth ; and we do not believe that any individual, who confides in the facts of astronomy, seriously rejects it. If such a person exists, we would gravely ask him for what purpose could so gigantic a world have been framed. Why does the sun give it days and nights and years ? Why do its moons throw their silver light upon its continents and its seas ? Why do its equatorial breezes blow perpetually over its plains ? unless to supply the wants, and administer to the happiness of living beings.

In studying this subject, persons who have only

a superficial knowledge of astronomy, though firmly believing in a plurality of worlds, have felt the force of certain objections, or rather difficulties, which naturally present themselves to the inquirer. The distance of Jupiter from the sun is so great that the light and heat which he receives from that luminary is supposed to be incapable of sustaining the same animal and vegetable life which exists on the Earth. If we consider the heat upon any planet as arising solely from the direct rays of the sun, the cold upon Jupiter must be very intense, and water could not exist upon its surface in a fluid state. Its rivers and its seas must be tracks and fields of ice. But the temperature of a planet depends upon other causes,—upon the condition of its atmosphere, and upon the internal heat of its mass. The temperature of our own globe *decreases* as we rise in the atmosphere, and *approach* the sun, and it *increases* as we descend into the bowels of the Earth and *go farther* from the sun. In the *first* of these cases, the increase of heat as we approach the surface of the Earth from a great height in a balloon, or from the summit of a lofty mountain, is produced by its atmosphere; and in Jupiter the atmosphere may be so formed as to compensate to a certain extent the diminution in the direct heat of the sun arising from the great distance of the planet. In the second case, the internal heat of Jupiter may be such as to keep its rivers and seas in a fluid state, and maintain a temperature sufficiently genial to sustain the same animal and vegetable life which exists upon our own globe.

These arrangements, however, if they are required, and have been adopted, cannot contribute to increase the feeble light which Jupiter receives from the sun; but in so far as the purposes of vision are concerned, an enlargement of the pupil of the eye, and an increased sensibility of the retina, would be amply sufficient to make the sun's light as brilliant as it is to us. The feeble light reflected from the moons of Jupiter would then be equal to that which we derive from our own, even if we do not adopt the hypothesis, which we shall afterwards have occasion to mention, that a brilliant phosphorescent light may be excited in the satellites by the action of the solar rays.

Another difficulty has presented itself, though very unnecessarily, in reference to the shortness of the day in Jupiter. A day of *ten* hours has been supposed insufficient to afford that period of rest which is requisite for the renewal of our physical functions when exhausted with the labours of the day. This objection, however, has no force. Five hours of rest is surely sufficient for five hours of labour; and when the inhabitants of the temperate zone of our own globe reside, as many of them have done, for years in the arctic regions, where the length of the days and nights are so unusual, they have been able to perform their functions as well as in their native climates.

A difficulty, however, of a more serious kind is presented by the great force of gravity upon so gigantic a planet as Jupiter. The stems of plants, the materials of buildings, the human body itself, would, it is imagined, be crushed by their own enormous weight. This apparently formidable objection will be removed by an accurate calculation of the force of gravity upon Jupiter, or of the relative weight of bodies on its surface. The mass of Jupiter is 1230 times greater than that of the Earth, so that if both planets consisted of the same kind of matter, a man weighing 150 pounds on the surface of the Earth would weigh 150 × 1200, or 180,000 pounds at a distance from Jupiter's centre equal to the Earth's radius. But as Jupiter's radius is *eleven* times greater than that of the Earth, the weight of bodies on his surface will be diminished in the ratio of the square of his radius, that is, in the ratio of 11 × 11, or 121 to 1. Consequently, if we divide 180,000 pounds by 121, we shall have 1487 pounds as the weight of a man of 150 pounds on the surface of Jupiter, that is less than *ten* times his weight on the Earth. But the matter of Jupiter is much lighter than the matter of our Earth, in the ratio of 24 to 100, the numbers which represent the densities of the two planets, so that if we diminish 1487 pounds in the ratio of 24 to 100, or divide it by 4·17, we shall have 312 pounds as the weight of a man on Jupiter, who weighs on the Earth only 150 pounds, that is, only double his weight—a difference which actually exists between many individuals on our own planet. A man, therefore, constituted like ourselves, could exist without inconvenience upon Jupiter; and plants, and trees, and buildings, such as occur on our own Earth, could grow and stand secure in so far as the force of gravity is concerned.

In removing difficulties, and answering objections such as these, we have conceded too much to the limited conceptions of the persons who have felt the one and adduced the other. To assume that the inhabitants of the planets must necessarily be either men or anything resembling them, is to have a low opinion of that infinite skill which has produced such a variety in the form and structure and functions of vegetable and animal life. In the various races of man which occupy our globe, there is not the same variety which is exhibited in the brutes that perish. Although the noble Anglo-Saxon stands in striking contrast with the Negro, and the lofty Patagonian with the diminutive Esquimaux, yet in their general form and structure, they are essentially the same in their physical and in their mental powers. But when we look into the world of instinct, and survey the infinitely varied forms which people the earth, the ocean, and the air;—when we range with the naturalist's eye from the elephant to the worm—from the leviathan to the infusoria—and from the eagle to the ephemeron, what beauty of form—what diversity of function—what variety of purpose is exhibited to our view! In all these forms of being, reason might have been given in place of instinct, and animals the most hostile to man, and the most alien to his habits, might have been his friend and his auxiliary, in place of his enemy and his prey. If we carry our scrutiny deeper into nature, and survey the infinity of regions of life which the microscope discloses, and if we consider what other breathing worlds lie far beyond even its reach, we may then comprehend the variety of intellectual life with which our own planets and those of other systems may be peopled. Is it necessary that an immortal soul should be hung upon a skeleton of bone, or imprisoned in a cage of cartilage and of skin? Must it see with two eyes, and hear with two ears, and touch with ten fingers, and rest on a duality of limbs? May it not reside in a Polyphemus with one eyeball, or in an Argus with a hundred? May it not reign in the giant forms of the Titans, and direct the hundred hands of Briareus? But setting aside the ungainly creations of mythology, how many *probable* forms are there of beauty, and activity, and strength, which even the painter, the sculptor, and the poet could assign to the physical casket in which the diamond spirit may be enclosed; how many *possible* forms are there, beyond their invention, which eye hath not seen, nor the heart of man conceived?

But no less varied may be the functions which the citizens of the spheres have to discharge,—no less diversified their modes of life,—and no less singular the localities in which they dwell. If this little world demands such duties from its occupants, and yields such varied pleasures in their discharge:—If the obligations of power, of wealth, of talent, and of charity to humanize our race, to unite them in one brotherhood of sympathy and love, and unfold to them the wonderful provisions for their benefit which have been made in the structure and preparation of their planetary home:—If these duties, so varied and numerous here, have required thousands of years to ripen their fruit of gold, what inconceivable and countless functions may we not assign to that plurality of intellectual communities, which have been settled, or are about to settle, in the celestial spheres? What deeds of heroism, moral, and perchance physical! What enterprises of philanthropy,—what achievements of genius must be required in empires so extensive, and in worlds so grand!

On a planet more magnificent than ours, may there not be a type of reason of which the intellect of Newton is the lowest degree? May there not be a telescope more penetrating, and a microscope more powerful than ours?—processes of induction more subtle,—of analysis more searching,—and of combination more profound? May not the problem of three bodies be solved there,—the enigma of the luminiferous ether unriddled,—and the transcendentalisms of mind embalmed in the definitions and axioms and theorems of geometry? Chemistry may there have new elements, new gases, new acids, new alkalies, new earths and new metals;—geology, new rocks, new classes of cataclysms, and new periods of change;—and zoology, mineralogy, and botany, new orders and species, new forms of life, and new types of organization,—all demanding higher powers of reason, and leading to a warmer appreciation, and a higher knowledge of the ways and works of God. But whatever be the intellectual occupation of the inhabitants of the planets, who can doubt that it will be one of their objects to study and develop the material laws which are in operation around them, above them, beneath them, and beyond them in the skies?

Under what suns, in what climates, and in what habitations, these planetary races are to live and move, may be conjectured from the place which they occupy in the system, and from the phenomena which they exhibit when examined by the telescope. It may not be in cities exposed to the extremes of heat and cold,—nor in houses made with hands,—nor in the busy market-place,—nor in the noisy Forum,—nor in the solemn temple,—nor in the ark which rests upon the ocean, that these feats of power and reason are to be performed. The being of another mould may have his home in subterraneous cities warmed by central fires,—or in crystal caves cooled by ocean tides,—or he may float with the Nereids upon the deep, or mount upon wings as eagles, or rise upon the pinions of the dove, that he may flee away and be at rest. Amid our bald and meagre conceptions of the conditions of planetary life, we may gather some ideas from the existences around us. In the cities and dwellings and occupations of the world of *instinct* in our own planet, rude though they be, we may trace the lineaments of the cities and dwellings and occupations of *reason* in another.

In continuing the argument for a plurality of worlds, it would be an unnecessary waste of time to enter into the same details respecting the analogy between the Earth and the other *three* superior planets of the system, as we have done with respect to Jupiter. In some, the analogies are more stringent than in others, but in all of them they are sufficiently numerous and powerful to command the assent of the unprejudiced mind.

In all the three planets, superior to Jupiter, namely, *Saturn*, *Uranus*, and *Neptune*, the direct light and heat of the sun is greatly less than that which falls upon Jupiter, being inversely proportional to the squares of their distances from the centre of their radiations ; but we have already seen, that in so far as vision and local temperature are concerned, the light of the sun may be as brilliant, and the temperature of the seasons as genial as they are upon our own Earth. An increased degree of sensibility in the nervous membrane of the eye, with an enlarged pupil, may give to light, geometrically feeble, a sufficient energy of sensation, while a different condition of their atmospheres, and a more ardent focus of internal heat, may maintain an agreeable temperature upon their surface.

The planet *Saturn*, encompassed with the extraordinary appendage of a ring, fitted to illuminate extensive portions of his surface, and encircled with eight moons to light him in the sun's absence, and revolving round him in months varying from the length of *one* day up to *eighty* days, has always been an object of peculiar interest to the astronomer, and of wonder to the ordinary student of nature. The plane of the ring, which we have described in the preceding chapter, is parallel to the equator, and has inequalities like mountains on its surface. The eight satellites of Saturn are placed at distances varying from 98,000 miles, the distance of the nearest from the planet, to nearly *two millions* of miles; and as the first five satellites are nearer Saturn than our moon is to the Earth, they will exhibit larger discs of light to the planet; and if, what is very probable, they are greatly larger than our moon, the firmament must exhibit a brilliant picture bespangled with large discs of light with a variety of phases, and spanned with the brilliant arches of the planet's ring. As the nearest of these moons, which is called *Mimas*, performs its revolution in *twenty-two hours and a half*, its phases must change from the slenderest crescent to the state of half moon in the course of *five hours*, and as its disc (if it has the same real size as our moon) must appear *two and a half* times larger, the boundary between the light and dark hemisphere will be seen actually advancing upon the body of the satellite. For the same reason, the motion of this satellite among the stars will be more perceptible than the movement of our stars and planets from their rising to their setting, produced by the diurnal motion of the Earth.[1]

In respect to the force of gravity upon the surface of Saturn, the analogy between it and the Earth is stronger than in the case of Jupiter. The density of Saturn is to that of the Earth as 24 to 100, or a little more than four times less, so that since the Earth is $5\frac{1}{2}$ times denser than water, the density of Saturn will be $1\frac{2}{5}$ths that of water. In like manner it may be shown that Uranus and Neptune have nearly the same density as water, and if we make the same estimation of the force of gravity upon the three superior planets, we shall find that in Saturn the force of gravity is a little greater than in the

[1] The appearance of the system of rings from the surface of Saturn, and of the phenomena which they produce in eclipsing occasionally and temporarily the sun, the eight satellites, and other celestial bodies, was for the first time accurately described by Dr. Lardner in a memoir published in the twenty-second volume of the *Transactions of the Astronomical Society* for 1853. Dr. Lardner has "there demonstrated that the infinite skill of the great Architect of the Universe has not permitted that this stupendous annular appendage, the uses of which still remain undiscovered, should be the cause of such darkness and desolation to the inhabitants of the planet, and such an aggravation of the rigours of their fifteen years' winter, as it has been inferred to be from the reasonings of the eminent astronomers already named, (Bode, Herschel, and Madler,) as well as many others, who have either adopted their conclusions, or arrived at like inferences by other arguments." "In short," Dr. Lardne adds, "the ring has no such character as would deprive the planet *of any essential condition of habitability*."—*Museum of Science and Art*, vol. i. p. 59.

Earth, and in Uranus and Neptune a little less, so that human beings like ourselves would experience no inconvenience from the greater or less force of gravity on these planets, and plants and trees, and architectural structures, of the same character with our own, would have the same strength and permanence.

In consequence of the rotation of Saturn upon his axis in about $10\frac{1}{2}$ hours, belts and streaks are seen upon his surface, produced, doubtless, like those in Jupiter, by equatorial currents like our trade winds. Variable masses of cloud diversify his surface, sometimes changing their place, and sometimes continuing so long in one position, that they reappear at one side of the planet's disc in the same place which they occupied five hours before when they disappeared on the other side of it.

In the two remote planets, *Uranus* and *Neptune*, the principal point of analogy with our Earth is, that they are lighted with moons, Uranus with *six* satellites, and Neptune with *one* or perhaps *two*, though we have no doubt that, like the other distant planets, he will be found to possess a greater number. The power of our best telescopes has not enabled astronomers to discover belts and clouds upon these two planets, and thus determine their daily motion. The oblate form of their discs, too, remains to be discovered ; but notwithstanding the absence of these points of analogy, the very existence of such large globes of matter revolving round the sun, and lighted up with moons, cannot fail to satisfy the unprejudiced and inquiring mind that they must have been created for some grand purpose worthy of their Maker. In the present state of our knowledge, it is impossible to conceive any other purpose but that of being the residence of animal and intellectual life.

There is one consideration in reference to the two remote planets, *Uranus* and *Neptune*, which some of our readers may regard as adding to the probability of their being worlds like our own. Some writers, or rather one, for we know of only one, have asserted that " however destitute planets, moons, and rings may be of inhabitants, they are at least vast scenes of God's presence, and of the activity with which He carries into effect everywhere the laws of nature, and that the glory of creation arises from its being not only the product, but the constant field of God's activity and thought, wisdom and power."[1] We shall not venture to ascertain how much more of God's glory is seen in the mere material structure of Saturn and his ring, and of Jupiter and his satellites, than it is in the minutest insect that lives but for an hour; nor shall we compare gigantic masses of self-luminous or illuminated matter with the smaller organisms which are daily presented to us. We shall admit that the vulgar eye even is delighted with the sight of planets made gorgeous by the telescope,—that astronomers are entranced by the study of their movements and their perturbations, and that the useful art of navigation may derive some advantage from the eclipses of Jupiter's satellites. The poet may rejoice in "the soft and tender beauty of the moon," and in the inspirations of the morning and the evening star. But where is the grandeur,—where the utility,—where the beauty,—where the poetry of the two almost invisible stars which usurp the celestial names of *Uranus* and *Nep-*

[1] *Of the Plurality of Worlds:* an Essay, p. 254.

tune, and which have been seen by none but a very few even of the cultivators of astronomy? The grand discoveries of Kepler, Newton, and Laplace, were made before these planets were known. They contribute nothing to the arts of terrestrial life: they neither light the lover to his mistress, nor mark by their silver ray the happy hours which are consecrated to friendship and to love. They are doubtless the abodes of life and intelligence—the colossal temples where their Creator is recognised and worshipped—the remotest watch-towers of our system from which His works may be better studied, and His glories more easily descried.

From Jupiter and the planets beyond him, we now proceed to the examination of Mars, Venus, and Mercury, and here we shall find analogies more or less numerous and striking with those of our own Earth. In this group of planets no moon or satellite has yet been discovered, and it is probable that none exists. An atmosphere of great height, and of a peculiar constitution, might in all of them supply the place of a moon. The density of Mars and Venus is very nearly the same as that of the

Earth, the former being 0·95, and that of the latter 0·92, while the density of Mercury is a little greater, being 1·12. As the diameter of Venus is nearly equal to that of the Earth, the force of gravity will be almost exactly the same; and in Mars and Mercury, whose diameters are only about one half that of the Earth, the weight of bodies are equally about one half of what they would be if placed upon our own globe.

In Mars, Venus, and Mercury, the length of the day is almost exactly twenty-four hours, the same as that of the Earth,[1] and in many other points the analogy with our globe is very striking. Continents and oceans, and green savannas, have been observed upon Mars, and the snow of his polar regions has been seen to disappear with the heat of summer. In Venus and Mercury their surface is variegated with mountain chains of great elevation, and but for the brilliancy of their discs, and the clouds which envelop them, the telescope would have discovered to us more minute details upon their surface.

1 The mean of the length of the day in these four planets, is within less than a minute of twenty-four hours. The days of Mercury, Venus, the Earth, and Mars, are respectively $24^h\ 5^m$; $23^h\ 21^m$; $24^h\ 7^m$, and $24^h\ 7^m$; the mean of which is $24^h\ 0^m\ 45^s$.

The planets of this inferior group are surrounded with atmospheres like our Earth. We actually see the clouds floating in the atmosphere of Mars. Venus and Mercury are surrounded with the same medium essential to life, and in Venus astronomers have even observed the morning and the evening twilight. These atmospheres are doubtless the means of tempering the great heat which Venus and Mercury receive from the sun ; and the same purpose may be answered by the absence of that internal heat which exists in the Earth, and which may be used to increase the temperature of the remoter planets. The intense light which Venus and Mercury receive from the sun may be adduced as an objection to the existence, upon these planets, of inhabitants like ourselves; but this objection is at once removed by the consideration that this intense light may be completely moderated either by a very small pupil, or by a diminished sensibility of the retina, or by a combination of both.

Such are the numerous analogies which subsist between our Earth and Mars, Venus and Mercury. They afford, as a popular writer observes, "the highest degree of probability, not to say moral certainty, to the conclusion, that these three planets which, with the Earth, revolve nearest to the Sun, are, like the Earth, appropriated by the Omnipotent Creator and Ruler of the Universe to races very closely resembling, if not absolutely identical with those with which the Earth is peopled."[1] After concluding his examination of the four exterior planets, Jupiter, Saturn, Uranus, and Neptune, the same able and candid writer concludes his elaborate chapter in these words:—

"We have thus presented the reader with a brief and rapid sketch of the circumstances attending the two chief groups of globes which compose the Solar system, and have explained the discoveries and striking analogies, *which taken together amount to a demonstration*, that in the economy of the material universe these globes must subserve the same purposes as the Earth, and *must be the dwellings of tribes of organized creatures* having a corresponding analogy to those which inhabit the Earth.

"The differences of organization and char-

[1] Dr. Lardner's *Museum of Science and Art*, vol. i. p. 23.

acter which would be suggested as probable or necessary by the different distances of the several planets from the common source of light and heat, and the consequent differences of intensity of these physical agencies upon them, by the different weights of bodies on their surfaces, owing to the different intensities of their attractions on such bodies, by the different intervals which mark the alternation of light and darkness, are not more than are seen to prevail among the organized tribes, animal and vegetable, which inhabit different regions of the earth. The animals and plants of the tropical zones differ in general from those of the temperate and the polar zones, and even in the same zone we find different tribes of organized creatures flourish at different elevations above the level of the sea. There is nothing more wonderful than this in the varieties of organization suggested by the various physical conditions by which the planets are affected."[1]

To this opinion of a mathematician and a natural philosopher, who has studied more than

[1] Dr. Lardner's *Museum of Science and Art*, vol. i. p. 63.

any preceding writer the analogies between the Earth and the other planets, we may add that of the most distinguished naturalist and anatomist of the present day, who speaks in an authoritative tone as representing the cultivators of that department of science which he has enriched with such important discoveries. "We have been accustomed," says Professor Owen,[1] "to regard the vertebrate animals as being characterized by the limitation of their limbs to two pairs, and it is true that no more diverging appendages are developed for station, locomotion, and manipulation. But the rudiments of many more pairs are present in many species. *And though they may never be developed as such in this planet, it is quite conceivable that certain of them may be so developed, if the vertebrate type should be that on which any of the inhabitants of other planets of our system are organized.*

"The conceivable modifications of the vertebrate archetype are very far from being exhausted by any of the forms that now inhabit the Earth, or that are known to have existed here at any period.

[1] *On the Nature of Limbs.* London, 1849, pp. 83, 84.

"*The naturalist and anatomist, in digesting the knowledge which the astronomer has been able to furnish regarding the planets and the mechanism of the satellites for illuminating the night season of the distant orbs that revolve round one common sun, can hardly avoid speculating on the organic mechanism that may exist to profit by such sources of light, and which* MUST EXIST *if the only conceivable purpose of these beneficent arrangements is to be fulfilled.* But the laws of light, as of gravitation, being the same in *Jupiter* as here, the eyes of such creatures as may disport in the soft reflected beams of its moons will probably be organized on the same dioptric principles as those of the animals of a like grade of organization on this *earth.* And the inference as to the possibility of the vertebrate type being the basis of the organization of *some of the inhabitants of other planets*, will not appear so hazardous when it is remembered that the orbits or protective cavities of the eyes of the vertebrata of this planet are constructed of modified vertebræ. Our thoughts are free to soar as far as any *legitimate analogy* may seem to guide them rightly on the boundless ocean of unknown truth. And if censure be merited for here indulging, even for a moment, in pure speculation, it may perhaps be disarmed by the reflection that the discovery of the vertebrate archetype could not fail to suggest to the anatomist many possible modifications of it beyond those that we know to have been realized in *this little orb of ours.*"

In referring to the doctrine of Plato respecting ideal archetypes, as thus revived by Professor Owen, the author of the *Essay on a Plurality of Worlds* pays the following just compliment to this eminent anatomist:—"If a mere metaphysician," says he, "were to attempt to revive this mode of expressing the doctrine, probably his speculations would be disregarded, or treated as a pedantic resuscitation of obsolete Platonic dreams, but the adoption of such language must needs be received in a very different manner when it proceeds from a great discoverer in the field of natural knowledge: when it is, as it were, forced upon *him* as the obvious and appropriate expression of the result of the most profound and comprehensive researches into the frame of the whole animal creation. The recent works of Mr. Owen, and especially one work *On the Nature of Limbs*, are full of the most energetic and striking passages, inculcating the doctrine which we have been endeavouring to maintain. We may take the liberty of enriching our pages with one passage bearing upon the present part of the subject.

"'If the world were made by an antecedent mind or understanding, that is, by a Deity, then there must needs be an Idea and Exemplar of the whole world before it was made, and consequently, actual knowledge both in the order of Time and Nature before Things. But conceiving of knowledge as it was got by their own finite minds, and ignorant of any evidence of an ideal archetype for the world or any part of it, they (the Democritic philosophers who denied a Divine Creative Mind) affirmed that there was none, and concluded that there could be no knowledge or mind before the world was, as its cause.'"

Before we read this passage in Professor Owen's work *On Limbs*, from which our essayist does not quote it,[1] for reasons which may be

[1] The quotation may be from Professor Owen's other works referred to by the essayist: to his work, for example, *On the Archetype of the Vertebrate Skeleton.*

conjectured, we never doubted that the accomplished professor did not believe in a plurality of worlds. Upon turning, however, to the volume itself, we found the beautiful passage which we have quoted in direct support of this great doctrine, which we may truly say, in the words of the essayist, "*proceeds from a great discoverer in the field of natural knowledge, and which was forced upon him* (Professor Owen) *as the obvious and appropriate expression of the result of the most profound and comprehensive researches into the frame of the whole animal creation.*"

But not only has the essayist dealt thus unfairly with his readers, he has treated Professor Owen in the same manner, by ascribing to him the first half of the preceding quotation, which the Professor quotes from "the learned Cudworth" in his own words, and which Cudworth gives as the opinion of "*the Democritic Atheists!*"

The observations of Professor Owen on ideal archetypes throw a real light on the subject of a plurality of worlds. If there be an ideal exemplar or archetype of vertebrate animals, and if the conceivable modifications of that archetype are far from being exhausted either in the animal forms which now inhabit the earth, or in the fossil remains of its primeval tenants, it is no idle speculation to suppose that the modifications may be developed in the vertebrate animals of other planets. We have a reason therefore, besides those of analogy and congruity, to believe in the existence of beings both intellectual and animal in the other regions of space. And as there must be an exemplar of intellectual as well as of physical man, may we not equally expect in the upper spheres modifications of mind which have not been exhibited in the terrestrial races? If the rudimentary wing of man be expanded into the soaring pinion of the eagle, may not those mental powers which are only rudimentary here, and which fail in grasping the infinite and the eternal, expand themselves in another planet, and approximate to that divine intelligence of which they are here but a feeble emanation?

Under the influence of such views, may we not conceive also the archetype of a world, the rudiments of which, imperfectly developed in our own globe, may have all its modifications exhausted in the planetary and sidereal domains? The uniformity in the general design of the bodies of animals, which Sir Isaac Newton compares with that "wonderful uniformity of the planetary system, which is the effect of choice," being thus compatible with an almost infinite diversity of parts, there may be the same numerous deviations from the archetype in the planetary world. "It may be allowed," says Sir Isaac Newton, "that God is able to create particles of matter of several sizes and figures, and in several proportions to space, and perhaps of different densities and forces, and thereby to vary the laws of Nature, and *make worlds of several sorts in several parts of the universe.*"[1] If all the structures of created things are

> "Parts and proportions of a wondrous whole,"

that *whole* is the sidereal universe, and those parts and proportions are the inhabited planets, satellites, and suns of which it is composed.

[1] *Optics*, edit. 1721, pp. 378, 379.

CHAPTER V.

THE SUN, THE MOON, AND OTHER SATELLITES, AND THE ASTEROIDS.

So strong has been the belief that the Sun cannot be a habitable world, that a scientific gentleman[1] was pronounced by his medical attendant to be insane, because he had sent a paper to the Royal Society, in which he maintained "that the light of the sun proceeds from a dense and universal aurora which may afford ample light to the inhabitants of the surface beneath, and yet be at such a distance aloft, as not to annoy them;"—that "vegetation may obtain there as well as with us,"—that "there may be water and dry land there, hills and dales, rain, and fair weather,"—and that "as the

[1] This gentleman was a Dr. Elliott, who was tried at the Old Bailey for shooting Miss Boydell. His medical attendant was Dr. Simmons, through whom he sent the paper for the Royal Society, and who referred the Court to the passage we have given as a proof of insanity. See *Edinburgh Encyclopædia*, Art. Astronomy, vol. ii. p. 616, or *Gentleman's Magazine* for 1787, p. 636.

light and the seasons must be eternal," the "sun may easily be conceived to be by far the most blissful habitation of the whole system." In less than ten years after this apparently extravagant notion was considered a proof of insanity, it was maintained by Sir William Herschel as a rational and probable opinion, which might be deduced from his own observations on the structure of the sun.

It is by no means necessary that those who believe in a plurality of worlds within the limits of our own system, should adopt the opinion that the *sun* which lights it, and the many satellites which light the primary planets, should be inhabited worlds. They form an entirely different class of bodies, and the arguments employed to shew that they may be inhabited are of a different nature from those analogies which so strongly apply to the primary planets. The Sun has a great function to perform in controlling the movements of the whole system. It is the fixed mainspring of the great planetary chronometers, without which they would stop, and rush into destructive collision. It is the lamp which yields them the light without which life would perish. It is the furnace which supplies the fuel without which every organic structure would be destroyed. Created for such noble purposes, we are led by no analogy to assign to it an additional function. The very same remark may be applied to our moon, and to all the satellites of the system. They are the domestic lamps which light the primary planets in the absence of the sun, and all of them, as well as our own, may exercise the other office of producing the tides of their oceans. It is quite otherwise with the primary planets: They have no conceivable function to perform but that of supporting inhabitants, unless we give them the additional one which they are all fit for performing, and which they perform so well, of becoming large lamps to their satellites; and if we invest them with this function, we obtain an argument in favour of the satellites themselves being inhabited.

We are willing therefore to admit, that analogy would fail us, were we to attempt by its processes to people the sun and the satellites with inhabitants. But analogy is not our only guide in such inquiries. The creations of the material world, whether they be of colossal or atomic magnitude, may have various and apparently contradictory purposes to perform ; and when we find that other purposes, not cognizable by our senses, or not demonstrable by our reason, may be promoted by such objects, we cannot resist the admission that such additional objects may have been contemplated in their creation. The great masses of ironstone in our earth, while they are a necessary part of its framework, and are intended mainly to supply man with the tools of civilisation, may have the tertiary or the secondary purpose of giving life to the needle of the compass, or of contributing to those great electrical and magnetical arrangements which exist on our globe. While the sun then and the satellites are primarily intended for the great purposes which they so obviously subserve, it is not unreasonable to suppose that they may also be the seats of life and intelligence.

After a skilful examination of the solar spots, Sir William Herschel has made it highly probable, if not certain, that the light of the sun issues from an outer stratum of self-luminous or phosphoric clouds, beneath which there is a second stratum of clouds of inferior brightness, which is intended to protect the solid and opaque body of the sun from the intense brilliancy and heat of the luminous clouds. In measuring, photometrically, the light of these three different structures, he found that the light reflected *outwards* by the clouds of the inferior stratum, was equal to 469 rays out of a 1000, or less than one-half of the light of the outer stratum, and that the light reflected by the opaque body of the sun below was only seven rays out of a 1000. Hence he concluded that the outer stratum of self-luminous or phosphoric clouds was the region of that light and heat which are transmitted to the remotest part of the system; while the inferior stratum, which is obviously of a different character from the other, is intended to protect the inhabitants of the sun from the blaze of the stupendous furnace which encloses them. In confirmation of these views, the faint illumination,—the *seven rays out of a thousand*, is a proof that the light of the outer stratum, and consequently its heat, must be extremely small on the dark body of the luminary which we see through what are called the solar spots, which are now universally admitted to be openings in the luminous stratum, and not opaque scoriæ floating on its surface.

It is curious to observe, how the conjectures in one science are sometimes converted into truths by the discoveries in another. Sir William Herschel, as we have seen, has stated it as the result of many observations, that the light of the sun does not proceed, as was almost universally believed, from a solid or liquid mass in a state of incandescence, or white heat, and the fact has been demonstrated by means of a beautiful optical discovery of M. Arago:—When a solid mass becomes luminous by being raised to a red or white heat, the rays which emanate from it in every direction do not proceed only from its outer superficies. They are radiated like those of heat from an infinite number of material points below the surface, and extending to a certain small depth. The rays which traverse this thin luminous film, have been found by M. Arago to be polarized, whereas, had they proceeded from an envelope of flame, they would not have exhibited this remarkable property. Now, M. Arago has also discovered that the rays which issue obliquely from the sun's surface are not polarized, and hence he is authorized to draw the conclusion confirming Sir W. Herschel's opinion, that the light of the sun issues from a gaseous envelope of flame, or self-luminous matter.

With this important result before us, we approach the question of the habitability of the sun, with the certain knowledge that the sun is not a red-hot globe, but that its nucleus is a solid opaque mass receiving very little light and heat from its luminous atmosphere. Sir William commences his argument by inquiring into the probability of the moon being inhabited.

"The moon," he says, "is a secondary planet, of a considerable size, the surface of which is diversified like that of the earth, by mountains and valleys. Its situation with respect to the sun is much like that of the earth, and, by a rotation upon its axis, it enjoys an agreeable variety of seasons, and of day and night. To the moon our globe will appear to be a very capital satellite, undergoing the same regular changes of illumination as the moon does to the earth. The sun, the planets, and the starry constellations of the heavens, will rise and set there as they do here, and heavy bodies will fall on the moon as they do on the earth. There seems only to be wanting, in order to complete the analogy, that it should be inhabited like the earth.

"To this it may be objected, that we perceive no large seas in the moon; that its atmosphere (the existence of which has been doubted by many) is extremely rare, and unfit for the purposes of animal life; that its climates, its seasons, and the length of its days, totally differ from ours; that without dense clouds (which the moon has not) there can be no rain—perhaps no rivers, no lakes. In short, that notwithstanding the similarity which has been pointed out, there seems to be a decided difference in the two planets we have compared.

"My answer to this will be, that that very difference which is now objected will rather strengthen the force of my argument than lessen its value: We find even upon our globe, that there is the most striking difference in the situation of the creatures that live upon it. While man walks upon the ground, the birds fly in the air, and fishes swim in water, we can certainly not object to the convenience afforded by the moon, if those that are to inhabit its regions are fitted to their conditions as well as we on this globe are to ours. An absolute or total sameness seems rather to denote imperfections such as nature never exposes to our view; and, on this account, *I believe the analogies that have been mentioned sufficient to establish the high probability of the moon's being inhabited like the earth.*"

Sir William Herschel proceeds to put the argument in another shape. He supposes that the inhabitants of the moon, and the other satellites, if they do exist, are of opinion that the Earth and the other primary planets are of no other use but as lamps, and "attractive centres to direct their revolution round the sun;" and he then asks, "if we ought not to condemn their ignorance as proceeding from want of attention and proper reflection?"

From these considerations Sir William thinks that the inhabitants of the planets ought to be wiser than we have supposed those of their satellites to be. "From experience," he adds, "we can affirm, that the performance of the most salutary offices to inferior planets is not inconsistent with the dignity of superior purposes; and in consequence of such analogical reasonings, assisted by telescopic views which plainly favour the same opinion, *we need not hesitate to admit that the sun is richly stored with inhabitants.*"

From the phenomena of variable stars which Sir William supposes to arise from their having spots, and revolving about an axis, he considers it as hardly admitting of a doubt that the fixed stars are suns; and he comes to the conclusion, that "if stars are suns, and suns inhabitable, we see at once what an extensive field of animation opens itself to our view." "It is true," he adds, "that analogy may induce us to conclude, that since stars appear to be suns, and suns, according to the common opinion, are bodies that serve to enlighten, warm, and sustain a system of planets, we may have an idea of numberless globes that serve for the habitation of living creatures. But if these suns themselves are primary planets, we may see some thousands of them with our own eyes, and millions by the help of telescopes; when, at the same time, the same analogical reasoning still remains in full force, with regard to the planets which these suns may support."[1]

The opinion of so distinguished an astronomer, and so excellent a man as Sir William Herschel, cannot fail to have much weight on a subject like this; but though we are desirous of strengthening rather than of controverting his arguments, there are yet some difficulties to be removed, and some additional analogies to be adduced, before the mind can admit the startling proposition, that the sun, moon, and all the satellites, are inhabited spheres. We may reject this opinion, and yet believe implicitly in a plurality of worlds.

In giving an account of these views of Sir William Herschel, Dr. Thomas Young[2] has remarked that "no clouds, however dense, could impede the transmission of the sun's heat to the parts below;" and that "if every other circumstance permitted *human* beings to reside upon

[1] *Philosophical Transactions*, 1795, pp. 65-69; and 1801, p. 296.
[2] *Elements of Natural Philosophy*, vol. i. pp. 501, 502.

it, their own weight would present an insuperable difficulty, since it would become nearly thirty times as great as upon the surface of the earth, a man of moderate dimensions weighing above *two tons.*" The first of these difficulties has certainly no weight. If the heat of the sun's rays is proportional to its light, which it must be if it is a flame, the darkness of the sun's nucleus becomes a measure of its coolness. Even a human being might live and breathe upon the solid nucleus under the heat which is indicated by *seven rays out of a thousand.* The second objection is equally inapplicable, because Sir William has never asserted, and never did believe, that the children of the sun were to be *human* beings, but, on the contrary, creatures "fitted to their condition as well as we on this globe are to ours."

It has been stated as an objection to the probability of the sun's being inhabited, that the whole firmament would be hid by the double atmosphere with which he is surrounded, and that the solar inhabitants would be excluded from all knowledge of the planets which he guides, and of the sidereal universe of which he is a part. This, however, is not strictly true. The planets and stars would be seen distinctly through the numerous openings in the solar atmosphere, and as the sun's surface is comparatively near to these openings, large portions of the heavens would be thus exposed to view. In many parts of our own globe weeks pass away without our seeing the sun or the stars, and it cannot be doubted that the inhabitants of the sun might study astronomy through the casual openings in the luminous cupola which encloses them.

The probability of the sun being inhabited is doubtless greatly increased by the simple consideration of its enormous size. Admitting, with Sir William Herschel, that the sun may have a temperature adapted even for human constitutions, it is difficult to believe that a globe of such magnificence, 88,000 miles in diameter, and upwards of one hundred times the size of our earth, should occupy so distinguished a place without intelligent beings to study and admire the grand arrangements which exist around them; and it would be still more difficult to believe, if it is inhabited, that a domain so extensive, so blessed with perpetual light, is not occupied by the highest orders of intelligence. In the material world with which we are connected, life everywhere meets our eye. It is virtually almost a property of matter, and therefore to conceive huge masses of matter, that are warmed and heated, destitute of life, is to do violence to our strongest convictions. Those who believe life to be the result of second causes, must believe in its universal diffusion ; and those who have the conviction, that into every living thing the Almighty must breathe its breath, will find it difficult to believe that the life which swarms around him on the earth, the ocean, and the air, of his own planet, has been denied to the other bodies of the system. Universal life upon universal matter is an idea to which the mind instinctively clings. Kingdoms without kings and subjects—continents without cities—cities without citizens—houses without families—ships without crews, and railway trains without passengers, are contingencies as probable as solar systems without planets, or planets without inhabitants.

To the arguments so well stated by Sir William Herschel in favour of his opinion that the moon is inhabited, some important considerations may be added. The moon certainly has neither clouds nor seas; but this is no reason why she may not have an atmosphere, and a precipitation of moisture upon her surface, sufficient for the support of vegetable life. The moon may have streams or even rivers that lose themselves, as some of our own do, either in the dry ground, or in subterranean cavities. There may be springs too, and wells sufficient for the use of man; and yet the evaporation from the water thus diffused may be insufficient for the formation of clouds, and consequently for the production of rain. The air may be charged to such a small extent with aqueous vapour, that it descends only in gentle dew, to be absorbed by vegetation, and again returned to the atmosphere. Even in our own planet there are regions of some extent where rain never falls,[1] and where the aqueous vapour in the atmosphere descends only in refreshing dew.

Although Sir John Herschel has stated that

[1] See Johnston's *Physical Atlas*.

there are no decisive indications of an atmosphere in the moon, yet he has given the following very ingenious theory of the climate of the moon, which implies the existence of an atmosphere, and even of *running water*. "The climate of the moon must be very extraordinary; the alternations being that of unmitigated and burning sunshine fiercer than an equatorial noon, continued for a whole fortnight, and the keenest severity of frost, far exceeding that of our polar winters, for an equal time. Such a disposition of things must produce a constant transfer of whatever moisture may exist on its surface, from the point beneath the sun to that opposite, by distillation *in vacuo*, after the manner of the little instrument called a *cryophorus*. The consequence must be absolute aridity below the vertical sun, constant accretion of hoar frost in the opposite region, and perhaps *a narrow zone of running water* at the borders of the enlightened hemisphere. It is possible, then, that evaporation on the one hand, and condensation on the other, may, to a certain extent, preserve an equilibrium of temperature, and mitigate the extreme severity of both climates;

but this process, which would imply the continual generation and destruction *of an atmosphere of aqueous vapour*, must, in conformity with what has been said above of a lunar atmosphere, be confined within very narrow limits."

In some of the principal craters, Sir John Herschel tells us "that there are *decisive marks of volcanic stratification*, arising from successive deposits of *ejected matter*, and evident indications of lava currents;" and he admits that "there are large regions perfectly level, and apparently of *a decided alluvial character*,"—conditions of the moon's surface, which demonstrate that there has been an atmosphere to promote combustion, and water to produce an alluvion. We do not understand how modern writers on astronomy have overlooked so completely the many arguments for the existence of an atmosphere in the moon, which have been almost universally admitted. Facts observed a century ago by astronomers distinguished for their accuracy, are not less important because they have not been observed by their successors. Volcanoes may have been seen in the moon in the 18th century, though they have not been observed in the 19th ; and a decided indication of atmospheric action to-day, will not be disproved by its invisibility to-morrow.

That volcanoes or burning regions have been observed in the dark portion of the moon's disc, cannot be doubted. In 1772, Beccaria, and in 1778, Ulloa, observed a bright white spot on the moon's disc. The spot observed by Ulloa and other three observers, resembled an opening in the moon ; but Beccaria was of opinion that this spot, as well as the one seen by himself, was the flame of a burning mountain. Various other persons have seen phenomena of the same kind ; but all doubt upon this subject was removed when so accurate an observer as Sir William Herschel announced the discovery of volcanoes in the moon. On the 4th May 1783, he perceived a luminous spot in the obscure part of the moon, and *two mountains which were formed from the 4th to the 13th of May !* On the 19th April 1787, he perceived "*three volcanoes in different places of the dark part of the moon.* Two of them were already nearly extinct, or otherwise in a state going to break out, which perhaps may be decided next lunation. The third shews *an actual eruption of fire*, or luminous matter." On the following day the volcano was burning with greater violence than the night before, and he found it equal to twice the size of the second satellite of Jupiter, and consequently, above three miles in diameter. Sir William observed that the eruption resembled a piece of burning charcoal. The existence of recent volcanoes may therefore be considered as a proof that the moon has an atmosphere.

Although Sir John Herschel broadly asserts, that in the occultations of stars and planets by the moon, there is no appearance whatever of an atmosphere ; yet we have many facts which stand in direct opposition to this statement. Cassini assures us, that he *frequently* observed the *circular* figure of Jupiter, Saturn, and the fixed stars changed into an elliptical one, when they approached either the dark or the illuminated limb of the moon. Mr. Dunn saw Saturn and his ring emerge from the moon's limb like a comet ; and M. Schroeter of Lilienthal, with fine telescopes, observed "several obscurations and returning serenity, eruptions, and other changes in the lunar atmosphere. The same astronomer discovered the twilight of the moon at the extremity of its cusps, and he found by measurement, that the inferior or more dense part of the moon's atmosphere was not above 1500 feet, or the *third* of a mile high, while the height of the atmosphere where it could affect the brightness of a fixed star, is not above 5742 feet, or not much more than a mile. Hence we see the reason why changes are only occasionally produced upon stars occulted by the moon. *Her atmosphere is greatly lower than her mountains.* When the stars, therefore, enter, or emerge from, behind mountains higher than her atmosphere, they are not affected by refraction ; and when behind mountains or level plains lower than her atmosphere, they are affected by the refraction of the superincumbent air.

It is evident, therefore, from all these facts, that in her volcanoes, active and extinct, in her twilight, and in her action upon immerging and emerging stars, the moon exhibits such proofs of an atmosphere, that we have a new ground from analogy for believing that she either has inhabitants, or is in a state of preparation for receiving them.

Had the moon been destined to be merely a lamp to our earth, there was no occasion to variegate its surface with lofty mountains and valleys and extinct volcanoes, and cover it with large patches of matter, that reflect different quantities of light, and give its surface the appearance of continents and seas. It would have been a better lamp had it been a smooth sphere of lime or of chalk. The existence of extinct volcanoes, the upheaval of lofty mountains, are proofs of a *progression in its physical history*—of a preparation, perhaps long ago made, for the reception of inhabitants. That it is not now preparing may be inferred from the absence of every appearance of change, since its surface has been studied by astronomers.

If it is probable, then, that the moon is inhabited, the same degree of probability may be extended to all the other satellites of the system. Their great distance from the earth prevents us from examining their surface ; but even without any indication of mountains and valleys, or of any forces that have disturbed or are still disturbing their surface, analogy compels us to conclude, that like all other material spheres, they must have been created for the double purpose of giving light to their primary planets, and a home to animal and intellectual life.

CHAPTER VI.

THE MOTION OF THE SOLAR SYSTEM ROUND A DISTANT CENTRE.

HAD our Sun, with all the planets and comets which he controls, been absolutely fixed in space, our system could have had no connexion with the other systems of the universe. The immense void which separates it from the stars, would have been regarded as the barrier which confined it. Astronomers, however, have not only placed it beyond a doubt that the Solar system is advancing in absolute space, but have determined the direction in which it moves, and within certain limits the velocity of its motion. This great cosmical truth, the grandest in astronomy, will furnish us with a new argument for a plurality of worlds.

The first astronomer who suggested the idea of such a motion, was the celebrated Dr. Halley,[1]

[1] *Phil. Trans.*, 1718, No. 355, i. v. vi.

who was led to it by comparing the places of Sirius, Arcturus, and Aldebaran, as determined by the observations of Hipparchus and Flamsteed. The French astronomers, Cassini and Le Monnier, noticed the same fact; but it is to Tobias Mayer[1] of Göttingen that we are indebted for a more complete examination of the subject. By comparing the places of eighty fixed stars, as determined by Roemer in 1706, with their places as observed by Lacaille in 1750, and himself in 1756, he found that the greater number of them had *a proper motion*, that is, a motion that could not be explained by any cause connected with the motion of our earth in its orbit, or upon its axis. In order to explain this motion, he suggested that it might arise from a progressive motion of the sun to one quarter of the heavens, in consequence of which the stars to which he was approaching would appear to recede from each other, while those in the opposite region from which he was moving would appear to approach one another; and he illustrated this idea by supposing a person walking in a field surrounded by trees, in

[1] *Opera Inedita*, 1775. *De Motu fixarum proprio*, pp. 77-81.

which case the trees to which he approached would appear to separate, or their distance to increase, while those which he left behind would appear to approach to one another, or their distance to diminish, the trees on his right and left hand preserving the same apparent distance from each other. This was the true cause of the proper motion of the stars, but owing to the imperfection of astronomical instruments in the time of Roemer, and even in Mayer's time, the observed proper motions did not correspond with his explanation of it; and he quitted the subject with the remark, that many centuries must elapse before the true cause of this motion can be explained.

Astronomy, however, was advancing more rapidly than its most ardent votaries imagined, and, before a single century elapsed, the motion of the solar system in space, as the cause of the proper motion of the stars, became a great truth, which commanded the assent and the admiration of every cultivator of astronomy.

Although Dr. Wilson[1] of Glasgow had pointed out, on theoretical principles, the probability

[1] *Thoughts on General Gravitation*, 1777.

of a progressive motion of the Sun, and Lambert[1] and La Lande[2] had deduced it from the idea, that the same mechanical impulse which gave the Sun its rotatory motion upon its axis, would displace its centre and give it a motion of translation, yet it was not till Sir William Herschel,[3] in 1783, analyzed the accurate observations of Dr. Maskelyne on thirty-five fixed stars, that a decided step was made in the investigation. He found that, in 1790, the solar system was advancing to the star λ in the constellation Hercules, or to a point in the heavens whose right ascension is 260° 34′, and north declination 26° 17′. By similar calculations, M. Prévost[4] found the right ascension of the same point to be 230°, with north declination 25°; and M. Klugel[5] made it 260°, with north declination 27°,—a result almost the same as that of Sir William Herschel.

It would be inconsistent with the nature of an Essay like this to enter into more minute details upon this subject. We shall, there-

[1] *Système du Monde*, pp. 152-158; and *Lettres Cosmologiques*, 1761, p. 126.

[2] *Mém. Acad. Par.* 1776, p. 513.

[3] *Phil. Trans.*, 1783, p. 247; 1805, pp. 233-256.

[4] *Mém. Acad. Berlin*, 1781.

[5] *Berlin Ephemeris*, 1789.

fore, give a tabular view of the results which have been obtained from places of the fixed stars, taken with the more accurate instruments of the present day, at the principal Observatories in Europe, and by the accomplished astronomers that direct them :—

Right Ascension and Declination of the point to which the Solar System is advancing.

Observers.	Right Ascension.		Probable Error.	North Declination.		Probable Error.	No. of Stars used.
Argelander I.	256° 25′·1	±	12° 21′·3	38° 37′ 2	±	9° 21′·4	21
Argelander II.	255° 9′·7	±	8° 34′·0	38° 34′·3	±	5° 55′·6	50
Argelander III.	261° 10′·7	±	3° 48′·9	30° 58′·1	±	2° 31′·4	319
Lundahl IV.	252° 24′·4	±	5° 25′ 3	14° 26′·1	±	4° 29′ 3	147
Otto Struve V.	261° 23′·1	±	4° 49′·9	37° 35′·7	±	4° 11′·8	392
Mean result VI.	259° 9′·4	±	2° 57′·5	34° 36′·5	±	3′ 24′·5	

The signs + and — in this table indicate that the probable error may extend on each side of the tabular number, by the quantities before which they are placed.

As the stars from which the preceding deductions have been made were those which are visible in the Observatories of Europe, it became interesting to determine the point to which the Solar system was moving, from the proper motion of the stars that are visible in the Southern hemisphere. This investigation has been lately made by our distinguished countryman, Mr. Thomas Galloway,[1] by means of eighty-one stars that were observed by Lacaille in 1751 and 1752, compared with those observed by Mr. Johnson at St. Helena in 1829–1833, and by our countryman, Mr. Henderson, at the Cape, in 1830, 1831. The result of this inquiry is, that the point of space to which our Sun is approaching is situated in

Observer.		R. Ascension.		N. Declination.	Prob. Error.
Galloway,	VII.	260° 0′·6	± 4° 31′·4	34° 23′·4	± 5° 17′·2
General Mean,	VIII.	259° 35′·0	± 3° 44′·4	34° 30′·0	± 4° 20′·8

Hence it appears, that the result obtained from the southern stars agrees with that from the northern ones, within 25′ of right ascension, and 7′ of declination, a coincidence so extraordinary as to amount to a demonstration of the great physical truth which it indicates.

But astronomers have not been satisfied with merely determining the direction to which the Sun, with all his planets, is advancing in space: They have calculated, within certain limits of error, the velocity with which they move! Assuming the parallax of stars of the first

[1] *Phil. Trans.*, 1847.

magnitude to be 0″·209, as determined by his father, M. Otto Struve finds that the angular value of the annual motion of the Solar system, if seen at right angles from the distance of such a star, is 0″·3392, with a probable error of 0″·03623; and taking the radius of the Earth's orbit as unity, we have $\frac{0''\cdot 3392}{0''\cdot 209}$ or 1·623, with a probable error of 0·229, as the annual motion of the Sun in space, reckoned in radii of the Earth's orbit. That is, taking 95 millions of miles as the mean radius of the Earth's orbit, we have 95 × 1·623 154·185 millions of miles, and consequently—

		English Miles.
The velocity of the Solar system,	.	154,185,000 in the year.
Do. do.	. .	422,424 in a day.
Do. do.	. .	17,601 in an hour.
Do. do.	. .	293 in a minute.
Do. do.	. .	57 in a second.

"Here, then," says M. Struve, senior, "we have the splendid result of the united studies of MM. Argelander, O. Struve, and Peters, grounded on observations made at the three Observatories of Dorpat, Abo, and Pulkova, and which is expressed in the following thesis:—'The motion of the Solar system in space is directed to a point of the celestial vault, situated, on the right line which joins the two stars π and μ *Herculis*, at a quarter of the apparent distance between these stars from π *Herculis.* The velocity of this motion is such, that the Sun, with all the bodies which depend upon him, advances annually in the above direction 1·623 times the radius of the Earth's orbit, or 33,550,000 geographical miles. The possible error of this last number amounts to 1,733,000 geographical miles, or a seventh of the whole value. We may thus wager 400,000 to 1 that the Sun has a proper progressive motion, and 1 to 1 that it is comprised between the limits of 38 and 29 millions of geographical miles.'"[1]

As there is no such thing in the heavens as a rectilineal motion, it is evident that the Sun, with all his planets and comets, is in rapid motion round an invisible body.[2] To that now dark and mysterious centre, from which no ray however feeble shines, we may, in another age, point our telescopes, detecting, perchance, the great luminary which controls our

1 *Etudes d'Astronomie Stellaire*, p. 108.

2 Professor Madler, without any very weighty reasons, makes the star *Alcyone*, the brightest of the Pleiades, the centre of the Sun's orbit.

system, and bends its path into that vast orbit which man, in the whole cycle of his race, may never be allowed to round. If the buried relics of primeval life have taught us how brief has been our tenure of this terrestrial paradise, compared with its occupancy by the brutes that perish, the grand sidereal truth which we have been expounding impresses upon us the no less humbling lesson, that from the birth of man to the extinction of his race, the system to which he belongs will have described but an infinitesimal arc in that grand cosmical orbit in which it is destined to revolve. If reason ever falters beneath the weight of its conceptions, it is under this overwhelming idea of time and of space. One round, doubtless, of this immeasurable path will the Sun be destined to describe. How long a journey has it been in the past! How brief in the present! How endless in the future!

We have thus endeavoured to give our readers an accurate idea of the nature and grandeur of this great cosmical movement, not merely because it will supply us with a new argument for a plurality of worlds, but because the author of the Essay already quoted, who denies this great doctrine, has completely misrepresented the great truth of the motion of the Solar system. Foreseeing its influence on the mind as an argument for more worlds than one, he has shunned the description of it even as a theory, and represented it to his readers as among "the conjectures of astronomers," and as founded upon "minute inquiries and bold conjectures," which he need not notice, as they "have no bearing on his subject."[1]

That the sidereal phenomena thus stigmatized are not conjectures but truths, *admitted by every astronomer*, our readers have seen. That they have a bearing on the doctrine of a plurality of worlds we shall endeavour to shew. The argument for a plurality of worlds may have two forms. It may embrace a new point of analogy between the inhabited Earth and any of the planets, primary or secondary; and since our Solar system is a system containing inhabitants, even if the Earth is the only planet that contains them, any point of analogy between that system and any other system of stars in

[1] *Of a Plurality of Worlds*, pp. 157, 158.

which there is a distinct movement of one star round another, becomes an argument for the existence of inhabitants, or of an inhabited planet in the other. It may have also a second form, namely, that which is called a *reductio ad absurdum*, that is, an argument in which it is shewn that the opposite opinion is an absurdity. The strictest truths in geometry have been considered as demonstrated by this species of argument, and it is still more applicable in the present case, where mathematical certainty cannot be reached, because there may be different degrees of absurdity, and we may have an *argumentum ad absurdiorem*, and an *argumentum ad absurdissimum*.

To illustrate this, let us suppose that, at a certain period in the history of astronomy, the Earth was believed to be the only planet that moved round the Sun. The astronomer of that day must have thought it strange that a sun 88,000 miles in diameter should be employed to light and to heat a planet only 8000 miles in diameter, as a smaller sun nearer the Earth would have been sufficient for the purpose. When Venus was discovered and found to be a planet of the same size as the Earth, with mountains and valleys, days and nights, and years analogous to our own, astronomers could not fail to think it probable that she was inhabited like the Earth ; and the *absurdity* of believing that she had no inhabitants, when no other rational purpose could be assigned for her creation, became an argument of a certain amount that she was like the Earth, the seat of animal and vegetable life. When Jupiter was discovered, and was found to be so gigantic a planet that it required *four* moons to give him light, the argument from analogy that *he* was inhabited became stronger, from the fact of his having moons, and the argument for a plurality of worlds became stronger also, because the analogy was extended to *two* planets. In like manner, every discovery of a new planet, either with new points of analogy, or with those previously existing in other planets, became an additional argument from analogy ; and when the system was completed with Saturn, Uranus, Neptune, and their numerous satellites, and when astronomers had discovered the existence of atmospheres, and clouds, and arctic snows, and trade winds in Saturn, Jupiter, Mars, and Venus, the argument from analogy attained a degree of force which it had not in the time of Fontenelle; and the absurdity of the opposite opinion that planets should have moons and no inhabitants, atmospheres with no creatures to breathe in them, and currents of air without life to be fanned, became a formidable argument which few minds, if any, could resist.

Considering then the Solar system as *stationary in space*, and unconnected with any other system, the argument for the existence of inhabitants on its planets, has a certain fixed value compounded of the argument from analogy, and the degree of absurdity which attaches to the idea of the planets being lumps of moving matter shone upon, and shining in vain. But when we have proved that this Solar system is revolving round some distant centre in an orbit of such inconceivable dimensions that millions of years might be required to perform one single round:—When we consider that this distant centre must be a sun, with attendant planets like our own, revolving in like manner round our sun, or round their common centre of gravity, the mind rejects, almost with indignation, the ignoble sentiment that man is the only being that performs this immeasurable journey, and that Jupiter, and Saturn, and Uranus, and Neptune, with their bright array of regal train-bearers, are but colossal blocks of lifeless clay encumbering the Earth as a drag, and mocking the creative majesty of heaven.

It is hardly necessary to illustrate these views by more familiar similitudes. The architect of a solar system stationary in space, and with but one of its smallest planets inhabited, may in some degree be likened to a sovereign, who, in sending a military colony to cultivate and defend an island in the Pacific, engaged *twenty-five* soldiers, *one* of whom was a light infantry man, who did all the honours and duties of the island, while the other *twenty-four* were tall and powerful grenadiers, who enjoyed themselves day and night upon merry-go-rounds, heated by genial fires, and lighted by brilliant chandeliers of gas, but performing no useful work, and doing no honour to their king. The Creator of the same solar system launched into an orbit of immeasurable circuit, and wheeling through ether with the velocity of fifty-seven miles in a second, may have some resemblance to a mighty autocrat, who should establish a railway round the coasts of Europe and Asia, and place upon it an enormous train of first-class carriages, impelled year after year by tremendous steam power, while there was but a philosopher and a culprit in a humble van, attended by hundreds of unoccupied carriages and empty trucks!

Since every fixed star, considered as the centre of a system, must have planets upon which to shine, we are furnished with a new argument from analogy, from the fact of our Solar system revolving round a similar system of planets, for as there is at least one inhabited planet in the one system, there must for the same reason be one inhabited planet in the other, and consequently, there must be more inhabited worlds than one—as many indeed as there are systems in the universe. This argument will be better understood when we have treated, in a future chapter, of binary systems of stars, to which the Newtonian law of gravity has been found applicable.

CHAPTER VII.

RELIGIOUS DIFFICULTIES.

It is as injurious to the interests of religion, as it is degrading to those of science, when the votaries of either place them in a state of mutual antagonism. A mere inference or a theory in science, however probable, must ever give way to a truth revealed ; but a scientific truth must be maintained, however contradictory it may appear to the most cherished doctrines of religion. In freely discussing the subject of a plurality of worlds, there can be no collision between Reason and Revelation. Christians, timid and ill-informed, have, at different periods, refused to accept of certain results of science, which, instead of being adverse to their faith, have been its best auxiliaries ; and infidel writers, taking advantage of this weakness have vainly arrayed the discoveries and infer ences of astronomy against the fundamental doctrines of Scripture. This unseemly controversy, which once raged respecting the motion of the Earth and the stability of the Sun, and more recently in reference to the doctrines and theories of geology, terminated, as it always must do, in favour of science. Truths physical have an origin as divine as truths religious. In the time of Galileo they triumphed over the casuistry and secular power of the Church ; and in our own day the incontrovertible truths of primeval life have won as noble a victory over the errors of a speculative theology, and a false interpretation of the word of God. Science ever has been, and ever must be the safeguard of religion. The grandeur of her truths may transcend our failing reason, but those who cherish and lean upon truths equally grand, but certainly more incomprehensible, ought to see in the marvels of the material world the best defence and illustration of the mysteries of their faith.

In referring to the planets of our own system, and to those which surround the fixed stars as suns, Dr. Bentley justly remarks, "that if any person will indulge himself in this speculation, he need not quarrel with revealed religion upon such an account. The Holy Scriptures do not forbid him to suppose as great a multitude of systems, and as much inhabited as he pleases. 'Tis true there is no mention in Moses's narrative of the creation of any people in other planets. But it plainly appears that the sacred historian doth only treat of the origin of terrestrial animals: he hath given us no account of God's creating the angels; and yet the same author in the ensuing parts of the Pentateuch, makes not unfrequent mention of the *angels of God.* Neither need we be solicitous about the condition of those planetary people, nor raise *frivolous disputes how far they may participate in* Adam's *fall or in the benefits of* Christ's *incarnation.* As if because they are supposed to be *Rational* they must needs be concluded to be *Men.*" He then goes on to shew that there may be "minds of superior or meaner capacities than human united to a human body," and "minds of human capacities united to a different body" . . . . . "so that we ought not upon any account to conclude that if there be rational inhabitants in the Moon or Mars, or any unknown planets of other systems, they must therefore have human natures, or be involved in the circumstances of our world."[1]

The doctrine of a plurality of worlds,—of the occupation of the planets and stars by animal and intellectual life, has been stated as "a popular argument against Christianity not much dwelt upon in books, but, it *is believed*, a good deal insinuated in conversation, and having no small influence on the amateurs of a superficial philosophy."[2] Although we have felt that such a difficulty might be made an objection to Christianity, we have neither met with it in books nor in conversation; but as it has been so prominently brought into view by Dr. Chalmers, and also by the author of the Essay *Of a Plurality of Worlds*, it is necessary to ascertain its value, whether it be urged by the infidel against the truths of Scripture, or by the Christian against the inferences of science.

"Is it likely," as Dr. Chalmers puts it, "says the infidel, that God would send His eternal

[1] *On the Confutation of Atheism*, &c., 1693, pp. 6-8.

[2] Chalmers's *Discourses*, &c. Discourse I.

Son to die for the puny occupiers of so insignificant a province in the mighty field of His creation? Are we the befitting objects of so great and so signal an interposition? Does not the largeness of that field which Astronomy lays open to the view of modern science, throw a suspicion over the truth of gospel history? and how shall we reconcile the greatness of that wonderful movement which was made in heaven for the redemption of fallen man, with the comparative meanness and obscurity of our species?"

In meeting this astronomical objection, Dr. Chalmers states that it consists of an *assertion*, which he denies, that Christianity was established for the exclusive benefit of our minute and solitary world, and of an *inference* or *argument*, that God would not lavish "such a quantity of attention on so insignificant a field." In denying the *assertion*, and maintaining that the inhabitants of other worlds may not have required a Saviour, Dr. Chalmers has obviously cut the knot of the difficulty rather than untied it. The assertion of the infidel, and the assertion of the divine, mutually destroy each other.

The *assertion* of the infidel, not his *inference*, has been maintained very generally by Christians themselves, and is indeed a difficulty which perplexes them. The assertion of the *divine*, on the contrary, is one which very few Christians will admit, and one which is opposed to the very system of analogy, which guides us in proving a plurality of worlds. If we argue that Jupiter, a planet with moons, must be inhabited because the earth which has a moon is inhabited, is not the infidel or the Christian entitled to say, that since the inhabitants of the Earth have sinned and required a Saviour, the inhabitants of Jupiter must also have sinned, and required a Saviour? To maintain the contrary opinion is not only against analogy, but it is a hazardous position for a divine to take when he maintains it to be probable that there are intellectual creatures occupying a world of matter, and subject to material laws, and yet exempt from sin, and consequently from suffering and death. A proposition so extraordinary we cannot venture to affirm. If it be true, the difficulty of the sceptic and the Christian is at once removed, because there can be no need of a Saviour ; and we are driven to the extravagant conclusion, that the inhabitants of all the planets but our own are sinless and immortal beings that never broke the Divine law, and are enjoying that perfect felicity which is reserved only for a few of the less favoured occupants of the Earth. Thus chained to a planet the lowest and most unfortunate in the universe, the philosopher, with all his analogies broken down, may justly renounce his faith in a plurality of worlds, and rejoice in the more limited but safer creed of the anti-pluralist author who makes the Earth the only world in the universe, and the special object of God's paternal care.

We must not, however, permit our readers to come to such a painful conclusion. Men of lofty minds and of undoubted piety have regarded the existence of moral evil as a part —a necessary part, we think, of the general scheme of the universe, and consequently as affecting all its rational inhabitants—the race of Adam on our own globe, and the races, perchance, more glorious than our own in the planets around us, and in the remotest system in space. When on the eve of learning the truth of his opinion, the illustrious Huygens did not hesitate to affirm, that it would be absurd to suppose that all things were made otherwise than God willed, and knew would happen; and that if we had lived in continual peace, and with an abundant supply of all the good things of this life, there would have been neither art nor science, and the human race would soon have lived like the brutes that perish. And with these views he comes to the conclusion, that the inhabitants of the other planets must be endowed with the same vices and virtues as man, because without such vices and virtues they would be far more degraded than the occupants of the Earth.

One of the most profound thinkers and elegant writers of the present day[1] has viewed this subject from a loftier eminence. "From the revealed record," he says, "we learn that the dynasty of man in the mixed state and character, is not the final one, but that there is to be yet another creation, or more properly *re*-creation, known theologically as the resurrection, which

[1] Mr. Hugh Miller, *Footprints of the Creator*, pp. 301-303.

shall be connected in its physical components by bonds of mysterious paternity, with the dynasty which now reigns, and be bound to it mentally by the chain of identity, conscious and actual ; but which in all that constitutes superiority, shall be as vastly its superior as the dynasty of responsible man is superior to even the lowest of the preliminary dynasties. We are farther taught, that at the commencement of this last of the dynasties, there will be a re-creation, of not only elevated, but also of degraded beings—a re-creation of the *lost.* We are taught yet farther, that though the present dynasty be that of a lapsed race, which at their first introduction were placed on higher ground than that on which they now stand, and sank by their own act, it was yet part of the original design, from the beginning of all things, that they should occupy the existing platform ; and that redemption is thus no after-thought, rendered necessary by the fall, but, on the contrary, part of a general scheme, for which provision has been made from the beginning ; so that the divine man, through whom the work of restoration has been effected, was in reality, in reference to the purposes of the Eternal, what He is designated in the remarkable text, '*the Lamb slain from the foundations of the world.*' Slain from the foundations of the world! Could the assertors of the stony science ask for language more express? By piecing the two records together—that revealed in Scripture, and that revealed in the rocks—records which, however widely geologists may mistake the one, or commentators misunderstand the other, have emanated from the same great author, we learn that in slow and solemn majesty has period succeeded period, each in succession ushering in a higher and yet higher scene of existence—that fish, reptiles, mammiferous quadrupeds, have reigned in turn, —that responsible man, 'made in the image of God,' and with dominion over all creatures, ultimately entered into a world ripened for his reception; but further, that this passing scene, in which he forms the prominent figure, is not the final one in the long series, but merely the last of the *preliminary* scenes; and that that period to which the bygone ages, incalculable in amount, with all their well-proportioned gradations of being, form the imposing vestibule, shall have perfection for its occupant, and eternity for its duration. I know not how it may appear to others; but for my own part, I cannot avoid thinking that there would be a lack of proportion in the series of being, were the period of perfect and glorified humanity abruptly connected, *without the introduction of an intermediate creation of responsible imperfection*, with that of the dying, irresponsible brute. That scene of things in which God became man, and suffered, *seems*, as it no doubt *is*, a necessary link in the chain."

At this startling result, our author finds himself on the confines of a mystery which man has "vainly aspired to comprehend." "I have," says he, "no new reading of the enigma to offer. I know not why it is that moral evil exists in the universe of the All-wise and the All-powerful; nor through what occult law of Deity it is that 'perfection should come through suffering.'" In the darkness of this mystery the best and the brightest spirits are involved; and our inability to fathom its depth we willingly acknowledge. But there are difficulties, which though we cannot solve them for others, we may solve for ourselves. An inferior intellect may disencumber itself of an incubus, which a superior one may be doomed for ever to bear. And as the physician, when he cannot achieve a cure, considers himself fortunate when he finds an anodyne, so the Spectre of Moral Evil may haunt the philosopher when the peasant has succeeded in exorcising it.

To exhibit the Divine attributes, and to display the Divine glory to an intellectual and immortal race, must have been the purpose for which a material universe was created. In his physical frame Man is necessarily subject to physical laws. The law of gravity "cannot cease as he goes by;"—and finite in his nature, and fallible in his reason, he can but feebly defend himself against the ferocity of animal life, the power of the elements, or the poison that may mingle in his cup. His high reason does not, in many emergencies, compensate for his inferior instinct. He is therefore helplessly exposed to suffering and death. The instincts of self-preservation and of parental affection give a magnitude and interest to whatever affects the safety and happiness of himself and his offspring.

He is thus placed in antagonism to his fellow-sufferers, and in the collision of interests and feelings, laws human and Divine are broken. Nor is this result less conformable to what we have regarded as the object and end of creation. In order to glorify God by a knowledge of His attributes, these attributes must be fully displayed. The power, and wisdom, and goodness of the Creator, are exhibited to us every day and every hour;—they are proclaimed in the heavens;—they are stamped on the earth;—life, and the enjoyments of life, display them even to the dumb, the deaf, and the blind. But in what region are we to descry the attributes of mercy, of justice, and of truth? In the abodes of happiness and peace, the idea of Mercy can neither have an object nor a name. Justice can be understood only among the unjust,—and Truth only among the untruthful. The moral attributes of the most High can be comprehended and emblazoned only among the cruel, the dishonest, and the false. His power, wisdom, and goodness, can be exhibited only in a material world, governed by the laws of matter; and man in his material nature must be subject to their operation and control. Though thus controlled and thus suffering, we feel that all is good and wise, and under this feeble gleam of reason there is light enough to show us—if we are disposed to have it shown—that the Spectre of Moral Evil has been conjured up by ourselves:

> All discord, harmony not understood:
> All partial evil, universal good.—POPE.

If we reject, then, the idea that the inhabitants of the planets do not require a Saviour, and maintain the more rational opinion, that they stand in the same moral relation to their Maker as the inhabitants of the Earth, we must seek for another solution of the difficulty which has embarrassed both the infidel and the Christian. How can we believe, says the timid Christian, that there can be inhabitants in the planets, when God had but one Son whom He could send to save them? If we can give a satisfactory answer to this question, it may destroy the objections of the infidel, while it relieves the Christian from his anxieties.

When, at the commencement of our era, the great sacrifice was made at Jerusalem, it was by the crucifixion of a man, or an angel, or a God. If our faith be that of the Arian or the Socinian, the sceptical and the religious difficulty is at once removed :—a man or an angel may be again provided as a ransom for the inhabitants of the planets. But if we believe, with the Christian Church, that the Son of God was required for the expiation of sin, the difficulty presents itself in its most formidable shape.

When our Saviour died, the influence of His death extended backwards, in the past, to millions who never heard His name, and forwards, in the future, to millions who will never hear it. Though it radiated but from the Holy City, it reached to the remotest lands, and affected every living race in the old and the new world. Distance in time and distance in place did not diminish its healing virtue.

> "Though curious to compute,
> Archangels failed to cast the mighty sum."

"Ungrasped by minds create," it was a force which did not vary with any function of the distance. All-powerful over the thief on the cross, in contact with its divine source, it was in succeeding ages equally powerful over the Red Indian of the west, and the wild Arab of the east. Their heavenly Father, by some process of mercy which we understand not, communicated to them its saving power. Emanating from the middle planet of the system, why may it not have extended to them all—to the planetary races in the past, when "the day of their redemption had drawn nigh;" and to the planetary races in the future, when "their fulness of time shall come?"

> "When stars and suns are dust beneath his throne,
> A thousand worlds so bought were bought too dear."

But, to bring our argument more within the reach of an ordinary understanding, let us suppose that our globe at the beginning of the Christian era had been broken in two, as the comet of Biela is supposed to have been in 1846, and that its two halves, the old world and the new, travelled together like a double star, or diverged into widely separated orbits. Would not both its fragments have shared in the beneficence of the cross,—the old world as liberally as the new,—the penitent on the shores of the Mississippi, as richly as the pilgrim on the banks of the Jordan. If the rays, then, "of the Sun of righteousness, with healing on His wings," could have shot across the void between our European and American worlds thus physically dissevered, may not all the planets, the worlds made by our Saviour himself, formed out of the same material element, and basking under the same beneficent sun, be equal participators in His heavenly gift?

Should this view of the subject prove unsatisfactory to the anxious inquirer, we may suggest for his consideration another sentiment, even though we ourselves may not admit it into our creed. If one man can expiate the crime of another by a punishment short of death, he may perform the same generous deed for a thousand. Should such a noble martyr consent even to give his life for his friend, by suffering a death from which science could revive him, he might expiate the crimes of thousands of his race. May not the Divine nature, which can neither suffer nor die, and which in our planet, *once* only, clothed itself in humanity, resume elsewhere a physical form, and expiate the guilt of unnumbered worlds?

In his zeal to overthrow the objection of the infidel, Dr. Chalmers has, we think, subjected it to a species of unnecessary torture. When the infidel thinks it unlikely "that God would send His eternal Son to die for the puny occupants of so insignificant a province of His creation," he does not mean that God cannot and does not take care "of the insignificant province" of the earth, because He has so many other nobler planetary kingdoms to govern. He means only that the mission of God's own eternal Son was too great a gift to the earth, and therefore one not likely to be given. The objection, indeed, which Dr. Chalmers puts into the mouth of the infidel is, in truth, an objection felt by the Christian; and the acute author of the Essay *Of a Plurality of Worlds*, seeing this mistake, actually treats it "not as an objection urged by an opponent of religion, but rather as a difficulty felt by a friend of religion." He considers it as a difficulty bearing on natural religion, and in this aspect he accepts of it as a difficulty, discusses its importance, and regards

Dr. Chalmers's reply to it as "well fitted to remove the scruples to which it is especially addressed." The difficulty is thus put by the anonymous author we have referred to :—

"Among the thoughts which it was stated *naturally* arose in men's minds when the telescope revealed to them an innumerable multitude of worlds besides the one we inhabit was this ;—*that the Governor of the Universe, who has so many worlds under His management, cannot be conceived as bestowing upon this earth, and its various tribes of inhabitants, that care which, till then, natural religion had taught men that He does employ to secure to man the possession and use of his faculties of mind and body, and to all animals the requisites of animal existence and animal enjoyment.* And upon this Chalmers remarks, that just about the time when science gave rise to the suggestion of this difficulty, she also gave occasion to a remarkable reply to it. Just about the same time that the invention of the *telescope* shewed that there were innumerable worlds which might have inhabitants *requiring the Creator's care* as much as the tribes of this earth do, the invention of the *microscope* shewed that there were in this world innumerable tribes of animals which had been all along enjoying the benefit of the Creator's care as much as those kinds with which man had been familiar from the beginning. The *telescope* suggested that there might be dwellers in Jupiter or in Saturn, of great size and unknown structure, who must share with us the preserving care of God. The *microscope* shewed that there had been close to us, inhabiting minute crevices and crannies, peopling the leaves of plants and the bodies of other animals, animalcules of a minuteness hitherto unguessed, and of a structure hitherto unknown, who had been always sharers with us in God's preserving care. The *telescope* brought into view worlds as numerous as the drops of water which make up the ocean ; the *microscope* brought into view a world in every drop of water. Infinity in one direction was balanced by infinity in the other. The doubts which man might feel as to what God would do, were balanced by certainties which they discovered as to what He had always been doing. His care and goodness could not be supposed to be exhausted by the hitherto known population of the Earth, for it was proved they had hitherto been confined to that population. *The discovery of new worlds at vast distances from us* was accompanied by the discovery of new worlds close to us, even in the very substances with which we were best acquainted, and *was thus rendered ineffective to disturb the belief of those who had regarded the world as having God for its Governor.*"

The difficulties, or "scruples," so distinctly stated in the preceding extract, whether we view them as an objection urged by an opponent of religion, as Dr. Chalmers does, or as a difficulty felt by the Christian, have, in our opinion, no existence; and, if they had, we consider the discoveries of the microscope as having no tendency whatever to remove them. It is a singular doctrine to maintain, that "the truths of natural religion" were ever exposed to danger by the discoveries of the telescope, or that astronomical truth ever excited the "doubts or difficulties," stated by our author, either in the minds of Theists or Christians of the most ordinary capacity. We have never read any works containing such doubts, nor listened to any conversations in which they were the subject of discussion. Amid the destructive convulsions of the physical world, even pious minds may have for an instant questioned the superintending providence of God. In the midst of famine, or pestilence, or war, they may have stood horror-struck at the scene. In the triumphs of fraud, oppression, and injustice, over honesty, and liberty, and law, Faith may have wavered, and Hope despaired ; but in no condition, either of the physical or the moral world, does the mind question the POWER of its Maker. The *omnipotence* of the Creator, and the exertion of it in every corner of space,—His care over the falling sparrow, and His guidance of the gigantic planet, are the earliest of our acquired truths, and the very first that observation and experience confirm. When Reason gives wisdom to our perceptions, omnipotence is the grand truth which they inculcate. Whatever the eye sees, or the ear hears, or the fingers touch,—every motion of our body, every function it performs, every structure in its fabric, impresses on the mind, and fixes in the heart the conviction, that the Creator is all-powerful as well as all-wise. Omnipotence, in short, is the only attribute of God which is universally appreciated, which scepticism never unsettles, and which we believe as firmly when under the influence of our corrupt passions, as when we are looking devoutly to heaven. All the other attributes of God are inferences. His omnipresence, His omniscience, His justice, mercy, and truth, are the deductions of reason, and, however true and demonstrable, they exercise little influence over the mind; but the attribute of omnipotence predominates over them all, and no mind responsive to its power will ever be disturbed by the ideas which it suggests of infinity of time, infinity of space, and infinity of life.

Is it conceivable that a Theist or a Christian of the smallest mental capacity could suppose that there are *degrees of omnipotence*, and imagine that the Almighty might be prevented, by the *many worlds under His management*, from taking care of the Earth and its inhabitants? If that Being who has made the living world which we see, can make millions of worlds, the same power which takes such care of its inhabitants that not a hair of their head can fall to the ground without His knowledge, can equally embrace in His capacious affections, and clasp in "the everlasting arms," all the families of the universe.

But even if we admit that such imperfect notions of omnipotence have been entertained, we deny that the discoveries of the microscope have the slightest tendency to correct them. Without alleging, as we might well do, that minds cherishing such notions of the Deity are incapable of appreciating the great truths, that there are "new worlds close to us;" that there is "a world in every drop of water;" and that "these worlds are as numerous as the drops in the ocean," we maintain that minds of the highest cast view the microscopic worlds as creations of an entirely different order from those disclosed by the telescope, and that such minds can never reason from *animalcular* to *intellectual* life. We admit, that the very same care which is required to preserve even an atom of invisible life, is necessary to maintain the gigantic forms of the elephant or the mammoth;

but ordinary minds, and those who think that their Maker may have *too much to do*, cannot comprehend, and therefore cannot receive, the doctrine that God takes care of mites and mosquitoes, and the other denizens of the microcosm at their feet,—of animalcules which they swallow in myriads at every act of deglutition,—which they suffocate in millions by every breath they draw,—and which, at every step, they trample relentlessly under their feet.

The religious difficulty has been presented in another form by the author of the Essay *Of a Plurality of Worlds*, but in a form so unintelligible to us, that we feel the greatest difficulty in comprehending it. Considering Man as an *intellectual*, *moral*, and *religious* creature, and having a progressive history in the development of these different conditions or privileges, as our author calls them, he sees a great difficulty in supposing that intellectual and responsible creatures analogous to man, can have a place in any of the other planets of our system. Viewing, he says, " the mode of existence of human species upon the earth as being *a progressive existence*, even in the intellectual powers and their results, necessarily fastens down our thoughts and our speculations to the earth, and makes us feel *how visionary and gratuitous it is to assume any similar kind of existence in any region occupied by other beings than men;*" and he elsewhere asserts "that if we will people other planets with creatures intelligent as man is intelligent, *we must not only give to them the intelligence, but the intellectual history of the human species.*" This assertion is supported by another assertion, "that the Earth and its *human* inhabitants are, as far as we yet know, *in an especial manner* the subject of God's care and government;" and from these and other assertions, in reference to man being under the moral government of God, and to the Earth being the theatre of the scheme of redemption, he comes to the incomprehensible conclusion, *that man's nature and place is unique*, and incapable of *repetition in the scheme of the universe!*

In order to test the accuracy of these assertions, and to discover what bearing they have upon the doctrine of a plurality of worlds, we must ascertain what has been, and what now is, the *progressive history* of man, as an *intellectual, moral,* and *religious* creature; and in what age, and in what regions of the globe it has presented, or does now present, that *unity of character and position which is incapable of repetition in the scheme of the universe.*

The history of the human species is the history of a variety of races in every stage of civilisation and barbarism, and the great majority of which have neither an *intellectual,* nor a *moral,* nor a *religious progressive* history. Progression has not been the character of the history of man. Without alluding to his primeval fall from his high estate, we have only to cast our eye over the globe, and look at the intellectual, moral, and religious catastrophes which it presents to us,—at ages of light and darkness,—at alternations of progress and decline,—at the highest civilisation sinking into the lowest barbarism. Mark those eastern lands, now involved in darkness, from which the beams of knowledge first radiated on mankind. Study the extinction of morality in many regions of the earth where its great lessons were first taught by our Saviour and His apostles; and above all, mark the total suppression of the Christian faith in European communities, where it has been displaced by a religion whose doctrines were preached by conquest, and whose decalogue was dictated by the sword.

May we not ask, then, which of these ever-changing conditions of humanity is that *unique* condition which cannot be repeated in the scheme of the universe? If it is the intellectual, moral, and religious race which is typified by Newton, and Shakespeare, and Milton, why may it not be the lowest in the scale of existence in some glorious planet, where the understanding, and the affections, and the imagination are to rise into higher forms of science, of poetry, and of philanthropy? Why may not the red Indian, the black negro, and the white slave, be the condition of intelligence in another sphere, —to be elevated to a nobler type of reason, and to a happier and a holier lot? And why may there not be an intermediate race between that of man and the angelic beings of Scripture, where human reason shall pass into the highest form of created mind, and human affections into their noblest development?

It is strange, and hardly credible, that the writer, whose opinion we are considering, should think it necessary that the planets, if inhabited, should be occupied by anything like man. Huygens, and Bentley, and Isaac Taylor, and Sir H. Davy, and Chalmers, have taken a different and a sounder view of the subject. The diversity in the races of man,—the immense and beautiful variety of forms and natures in the world of instinct,—and the countless beauties and differences in the structures and properties of vegetable and mineral bodies, whether of the ancient or the present earth, all concur in satisfying us that there will be the same diversity in the occupants and in the productions of the planetary regions.—Why may not the intelligence of the spheres be ordained for the study of regions and objects, unstudied and unknown on earth? Why may not labour have a better commission than to earn its bread by the sweat of its brow? Why may it not pluck its loaf from the bread-fruit tree, or gather its manna from the ground, or draw its wine from the bleeding vessels of the vine, or inhale its anodyne breath from the paradise gas of its atmosphere?

But whatever races be in the celestial spheres, we feel sure that there must be *one*, among whom there are no man-eaters—no parent slayers—no widow burners—no infant killers—no heroes with red hands—no sovereigns with bloody hearts—and no statesmen who, by leaving the people untaught, educate them for the scaffold. In the decalogue of that community will stand pre-eminent, in letters of burnished gold, the highest of all social obligations—

THOU SHALT NOT KILL,

—neither for territory, for fame, for lucre, nor for crime,—neither for food, nor for raiment, nor for pleasure. The lovely forms of life, and sensation, and instinct, so delicately fashioned by the master hand, shall no longer be destroyed and trodden under foot, but be objects of unceasing love and admiration,—the study of the philosopher, the theme of the poet, and the auxiliaries and companions of man.

The difficulties we have been considering, in so far as they are of a religious character, have been very unwisely introduced into the question of a plurality of worlds. We are not entitled to remonstrate with the sceptic, but we venture to doubt the soundness of that philosopher's judgment, who thinks that the truths of natural religion are affected by a belief in planetary races, and the reality of that Christian's faith who considers it to be endangered by a belief that there are other worlds than his own.

CHAPTER VIII.

SINGLE STARS AND BINARY SYSTEMS.

IF we suppose ourselves placed successively on Mars, Jupiter, Saturn, Uranus, and Neptune, the Sun will successively appear smaller and smaller, and at Neptune it will still have a round and distinctly defined disc. At greater distances beyond our system the disc of the Sun would be seen only through a telescope, and all the planets, except Jupiter and Saturn, will have disappeared. At a greater distance still they will vanish in succession, and before we cross the immense void which lies between our system and the nearest system of the stars, our Sun will be seen as a single star twinkling in the sky. All his planets, primary and secondary, and all his comets, will have disappeared in the distance.

Hence we are led to believe that the fixed

stars are the suns of other systems, whose planets are invisible from their distance. As no change of place has been observed in *single* fixed stars, excepting that which is common to them all, and arises from the motion of our system, we are entitled to consider these single stars as the centres of systems like our own; to suppose them without planets, and to be merely globes of light and heat, would be contrary to analogy as well as to reason. We know that there is one star in the universe surrounded by planets, and one of these planets inhabited; and when we see another single star equal, if not greater in brilliancy, we are entitled to regard it as the centre of a system, and that system with at least one inhabited planet. This conclusion is rendered more probable by estimates which have been made of the comparative brightness and probable magnitude of some of the single fixed stars.[1]

[1] With the view of shewing that analogy does not lead us to believe that stars, considered as suns, are not surrounded with planets, the author of the Essay *Of a Plurality of Worlds*, has, in a note, quoted in the following manner, a passage from Humboldt, as confirming his opinion.

"Humboldt," says he, "regards the force of analogy as tending in the opposite direction. 'After all,' he asks, (*Cosmos* III. 373,) 'is the assumption of satellites to be fixed stars so absolutely necessary? If we were to begin from the outer planets, Jupiter, &c., analogy might seem

These estimates have been obtained from measures of the brightness and distance of a small number of stars. The distance of a star is obtained from what is called its *Parallax*,—namely, its change of place in the heavens when seen from the two most distant points of the earth's orbit, or, what is the same thing, the angle subtended at the star by lines drawn from it to the two most distant points of the earth's orbit, which are separated by a length of 190 millions of miles. The following are almost the only correct measures of parallax which have been obtained by the fine instruments, and the accurate observations of modern astronomers.

to require that all planets have satellites. But yet this is not true, for Mars, Venus, and Mercury, have no satellites, to which we may further add the *twenty-three* planetoids. In this case there is a much greater number of bodies which have not satellites than which have them."—P. 162, *note*.

There is certainly some singular confusion of ideas either in Humboldt or his commentator, or in both. Nobody ever maintained that the stars have *satellites*. They are supposed only to have planets, and if any person should maintain that these primary planets have satellites, the observation of Humboldt would be quite applicable, because analogy tells us that it is as likely that they have no satellites as that they have them, or rather, as in the Solar system, that some may have satellites, and others not. The author of the Essay, however, means by satellites not moons, but primary planets, and he has certainly made an extraordinary blunder, when he infers that there may be no planets round the star suns, because there are planets without satellites. If there had not been in the Solar system a single satellite, analogy could never have led us to conclude that there were no primary planets round the stars.

α Centauri, . .	0″·913	Henderson and Maclean.
61 Cygni, . .	0″·374	Bessel.
α Lyræ, . .	0″·207	Peters.
Sirius, . .	0″·230	Henderson.
Arcturus, . .	0″·127	Peters.
Pole Star, . .	0″·106	Peters.
Capella, . .	0″·046	Peters.

The star *a Centauri*, which is the nearest to our system, has been found to be about two-and-a-half times brighter than our Sun, and the star *Sirius*, the brightest in the heavens, has been found to be four times brighter than *a Centauri*; but the distance of *Sirius* is four times greater than that of *a Centauri*, and therefore the intrinsic brightness of Sirius is sixty-three times greater than that of our Sun. A luminary like this, so resplendent in its brightness, and so gigantic, doubtless, in its magnitude, was surely not planted in space to shed its light and its heat upon nothing. The star *Capella*, too, a star of the first magnitude, is *twenty* times more remote than *a Centauri*, and must, like Sirius, be a sun of enormous size. Can we doubt, then, that every *single* star, shining by its own native light, is the centre of a planetary system like our own, the lamp that lights, the stove that heats, and the power that guides in their orbits inhabited worlds like our own?

A great number of the fixed stars, some of which are of the first magnitude, like *Castor*, have been found, by the fine telescopes of modern times, to be *double*, and, from observations made at different dates, one of the stars has been found to revolve round the other, and to form what is called a *Binary System*; —that is, a system in which one sun with its system of planets revolves round another sun with its system of planets, or rather round the centre of gravity of both. The two suns of course are only seen, owing to the great distance of their respective systems from us; but no person can believe that two suns could be placed in the heavens for no other purpose than to revolve round their common centre of gravity.

The orbits of no fewer than *thirteen* double stars, or *binary systems*, first discovered by Sir William Herschel, have been calculated by Sir John Herschel, Savary, Madler, Captain Smyth, Hind, Encke, and Jacob, and there can be no doubt that the Newtonian law of gravity extends to those bodies. The periods of these systems extend from 31½ years, which is that of ζ *Herculis*, to 737 years, which is that of σ *Coronæ* B, both of which were calculated by Madler; but the most interesting is γ *Virginis*, whose revolution, as computed by Sir John Herschel, is 182 years. This system is a very interesting one. The two stars which compose it are nearly equal, and, according to Struve, slightly variable, the two being sometimes equal in brightness, and sometimes unequal. Dr. Bradley had observed, in 1718, the apparent direction of the line joining the two stars. In 1780, Sir William Herschel observed the distance of the two stars to be 5″·7, which regularly diminished till 1836, when the two appeared perfectly round, like a single star when seen by the finest telescopes. After 1836 the stars separated, and their distance is now more than 2″. The change in their angular motion, that is, in the direction of the line joining them, has been equally remarkable, and was as follows :—

In 1783,	½°	per annum.
1830,	5°	...
1834,	20°	...
1835,	40°	...
1836,	70°	...

The star of the shortest period, namely, ζ *Herculis*, has performed two revolutions since it was first discovered, and the small star has been twice completely eclipsed by the large one. Other three double stars, η *Coronæ*, ζ *Cancri*, and ξ *Ursæ Majoris*, have performed more than one complete revolution in their orbits, and there can be no doubt that these motions are the result of centripetal forces varying inversely as the square of the distance. "We have the same evidence, indeed," says Sir John Herschel, "of their motions about each other that we have of those of Uranus and Neptune about the Sun; and the correspondence of their calculated and observed places in such very elongated ellipses must be admitted to carry with it proof of the prevalence of the Newtonian law of gravity in their systems, of the very same nature and agency as that of the calculated and observed places of comets round the central body of our own."

In reference to systems like these, the argument in favour of their being surrounded with inhabited planets, is stronger than in the case of single systems. We have in this case a decided visible movement of one of the stars round the other: We have also elliptical orbits described by the same law of force which guides our own Earth and the other planets in the Solar system; and though, upon the same principles which led us to agree with Sir William Herschel in thinking that our own Sun may be inhabited, we may believe the two suns of binary systems to be inhabited, yet it is more reasonable and consistent with analogy to believe that each of them is accompanied, as Sir John Herschel remarks, "with its train of planets and their satellites, closely shrouded from our view by the splendour of their respective suns, and crowded into a space bearing hardly a greater proportion to the enormous interval which separates *them* than the distances of the satellites of our planets from their primaries bear to their distances from the Sun himself. A less distinctly characterized subordination would be incompatible with the stability of their systems, and with the planetary nature of their orbits. Unless closely nestled under the protecting wing of their immediate superior, the sweep of their other sun, in its perihelion passage round their own, might carry them off, or whirl them into orbits utterly incompatible with the *conditions necessary for* the existence of their inhabitants."[1]

From the motion of our own system round a distant centre, it is highly probable that our sun is one of a binary system, although its partner has not been discovered. If Madler's speculation is correct, our sun and the star *Alcyone* form a binary system, and therefore since our sun is attended with planets, and one of these inhabited, we are entitled by analogy to conclude that all other binary systems have planets at least round one of their suns, and that one of these planets is the seat of vegetable and animal life.

The number of double stars is very great, and also of multiple stars, and groups and clusters; but ages must elapse before astronomers can determine the relation in which the stars that compose each system or group are related to one another. In the meantime we are compelled to draw the conclusion, that

[1] *Outlines of Astronomy*, § 846.

wherever there is a sun, a gigantic sphere, shining by its own light, and either fixed or moveable in space, there must be a planetary system, and wherever there is a planetary system, there must be life and intelligence.

The number of fixed stars, though greater than the atoms of sand on the sea shore, forms no argument to the instructed mind against their being occupied by living beings. When the philosopher, with his microscope, discovered that the polieschiefer of Bohemia, and chalk and solid marble, consisted almost wholly of the remains of animal life, the world stood aghast at the intelligence:—They were still more astonished at the statement that many thousands of millions of such infusorial animals could be counted in a cubic inch of their lifeless remains; but their faith was more severely taxed when they learned that whole strata and hills were formed of these fossil skeletons.[1] In like manner we are at first startled with the deduction that the planets of our own system

[1] Ehrenberg found that one cubic inch of the Bilin polieschiefer slate contains 41,000 millions of these microscopic infusorial animals, called *Galionella distans,* and that a cubic inch of the same material contains above one billion 750,000 millions of distinct individuals of *Galionella ferruginea.*

are the seats of intellectual life. We marvel still more at the announcement that the systems of the stars are planetary, and inhabited like our own ; and our faltering reason utterly fails us when called upon to believe that *even the nebulæ* must be surrendered to life and reason. Wherever there is matter there must be Life ; Life Physical to enjoy its beauties—Life Moral to worship its Maker, and Life Intellectual to proclaim His wisdom and His power.

CHAPTER IX.

CLUSTERS OF STARS AND NEBULÆ.

AMONG the bodies of the sidereal universe, astronomers have from the earliest ages recognised the existence of *clusters of stars* and of *nebulæ*. The *Milky Way* indicates by its name that it is of a *nebular* character ; but a nebula, properly so called, is a limited space of light, of various forms and various degrees of brightness in its different parts. Sir William Herschel was the first astronomer who observed this class of phenomena systematically, and who divided the bodies which compose it into *six* classes,[1] namely,

1. *Clusters of stars*, in which each star is distinctly seen.

2. *Resolvable Nebulæ*, or such as *excite a*

[1] We omit the other three classes of planetary nebulæ, stellar nebulæ, and nebular stars, as unconnected with our subject.

suspicion that they consist of stars, and which a higher magnifying power *may be expected* to resolve into separate stars.

3. *Nebulæ*, properly so called, in which *there is no appearance whatever of stars.*

It is very obvious that the language used in the above classification, is intended to support the theory that there is such a thing in the sidereal space as *real nebulous matter*, or star dust, as it has been almost jocularly called, contradistinguished from a nebulous mass of identically the same appearance which the telescope has resolved into separate stars. The phrases which we have put in italics are certainly incorrect, because *any appearance*, or *any expectation* of a nebula not being resolvable, is proved to have been erroneous the moment it is resolved. The classification of nebulæ, therefore, should have been, 1. Nebulæ that the telescope *had resolved;* and, 2. Nebulæ that the telescope *had not resolved.*

Sir William Herschel believed in the existence of purely nebulous matter, or star dust, and what has been called the *theory of sidereal aggregation ;* and since his time it has been made the basis of wild and extravagant speculations equally incompatible with physical and revealed truth. It is, therefore, of some importance that we should succeed in convincing the reader that the existence of nebulæ not yet resolved, is no proof of the existence of star dust, and that we are entitled to conclude that such nebulæ are clusters of stars,—that each star is the sun of a planetary system, and each planet the residence of life and reason. Each nebula, in short, corresponds with our hill of microscopic infusorial animals,—each system with a cubic inch of its materials, and each planet with a cubic line. If we have seen with our own eyes in the microscope the individual animal—only the *ten thousandth* part of an inch in size, and if we have seen the hill which is an accumulation of them, need we wonder at nebulæ being stars,—at stars being suns,—and at planets being inhabited ?

As it is now an astronomical fact that nebulæ, which Sir William Herschel, with his finest telescopes, could not resolve, and which had *no appearance* whatever of being resolvable, have been resolved into distinct stars by the magnificent reflectors of Lord Rosse, we are enabled without any hypothetical statements to place the question of the existence of star dust or purely nebulous matter, in its proper aspect;—that is, we can assign a satisfactory reason to the reader for considering every nebula in the heavens as a cluster of stars which is likely to be resolved by telescopes superior to those of Lord Rosse.

For this purpose, let us suppose *seven clusters of stars* placed at seven different distances in space, and all of which were regarded as nebulæ before the invention of the telescope. When Galileo applied his little telescope to nebula No. 1, or the nearest of the seven, he observed it to consist of separate stars so distinct that he could count them, and he concluded from their having no parallax, and being at an enormous distance, that each was a gigantic sun. Galileo tries in vain to resolve No. 2, which is at a greater distance, and therefore though he thought that a better telescope would resolve it and all the other five, they still remained as nebulæ in the heavens. Sir Isaac Newton, however, nearly a century later, applies his little reflecting telescope to No. 2, and succeeds in resolving it, while he fails in resolving five, but he believes, on better evidence than Galileo, that the other five nebulæ are clusters of stars. Hadley with his fine Gregorian reflector easily resolves No. 3; James Short, in like manner, resolves No. 4; Sir William Herschel No. 5; and Lord Rosse No. 6. All these astronomers, after the observation of Galileo, believed that all the seven nebulæ were clusters of stars, each of them with increasing evidence; and Lord Rosse, that No. 7 was a cluster on stronger evidence than the rest. Lord Rosse, however, fails in resolving No. 7 with his largest instrument, but he does not scruple to express his conviction, nay, he cannot help being convinced, that, with a telescope, even a little larger than his own, but certainly with one twice its size, which may be the work of another century,—the *seventh* nebula will also be resolved. The same reasoning which we have used for *seven* nebulæ is applicable to *seventy* or *seven hundred*, or even *seven thousand;* and the conclusion is inevitable, though the evidence of demonstration is wanting, that all nebulæ are clusters of stars.

There is another point of view from which we may regard this subject. Purely nebulous matter, such as that which composes comets' tails, and still more that which, in the form of the *zodiacal* light, is, without reason, called the sun's atmosphere, must consist of the minutest particles, so minute that they do not retard Venus or Mercury while they pass through the so-called atmosphere of the sun, which is alleged to extend beyond their orbits. Now, if No. 6 was considered a nebula before it was resolved, it must have been regarded as consisting of *minute particles* of star dust, whereas, the moment it was resolved, it consisted of separate suns, each of which was probably greater than our own. Is it possible that self-luminous star dust, at such an infinite distance from us in space, and so rare as to be like a non-resisting medium, could send to our system a light as intense as that which is emitted by the same nebula considered as a cluster of suns! If the resolved nebula No. 6, and the unresolved nebula No. 7, have the same appearance and the same intensity of light, is it not certain that the latter must have the same constitution as the former, that is, must consist of stars?

There is another aspect of this question, which, as it has not yet been the subject of discussion, may deserve the attention of astronomers. It is not only quite possible, but we think it is almost certain, that in the distant sidereal spaces there may be nebulæ, which, though really clusters of stars, never can be resolved. Our hypothetical nebula, for example, No. 7, may not only resist the telescopes of ages to come, but may be incapable of resolution by *telescopes of infinite power and infinite perfection.* Unless when a star is in the zenith, the rays by which we see it are bent and dispersed by the refraction of the atmosphere, and as our atmosphere is not a homogeneous medium, a star may be so infinitely minute from its distance, that though its light makes its way undisturbed in its journey of a thousand years, it may be so treated in its passage through our atmosphere that an image of it cannot be formed in the focus of a telescope, considered as absolutely perfect. An increase of magnifying power would only increase the effect produced by the atmosphere. In the case of a single star thus acted upon, it would be invisible from the diffusion of its light, while in the case of clusters the cluster would continue to appear a nebula, the diffused light of each star being mingled with that of its neighbours.

The interesting discovery made by Lord Rosse of what is called *spiral nebulæ*, where the nebulous matter may be considered as having been thrown off by some singular cause from the centre of the nebulæ, may be regarded as hostile to the opinion that such nebulæ are composed of separate stars. An appearance which *might* be caused by motion, is certainly no ground for believing that motion caused it. Various forms have been observed in nebulæ. They are globular and oval, with all degrees of ellipticity, from a circle to a straight line; and Sir John Herschel remarks it as " a fact, connected in some very intimate manner with the dynamical condition of their subsistence," that they are more difficult of resolution than globular nebulæ. Now these linear nebulæ, which Sir John Herschel thinks are flat ellipsoids seen edgewise, though they may, by speculators in star dust, be regarded as spheres thrown into their ellipsoidal state by a very rapid rotation round their lesser axis, yet have no such origin, because they have been resolved into stars. In like manner the nebulæ called *annular*, which have the form of rings, might be regarded by the same persons as produced from a still more rapid rotation, which we know from the beautiful experiments of M. Plateau, will convert a sphere into a ring; but that this is not their origin is proved by their consisting of stars. The beautiful nebula, for example, between β and γ *Lyræ*, has the appearance of "a flat oval solid ring."

"The axes of the ellipse," according to Sir John Herschel, "are to each other in the proportion of about 4 to 5, and the opening occupies about half, or rather more than half the diameter. The central vacuity is not quite dark, but is filled in with faint nebulæ like a gauze stretched over a hoop. The principal telescopes of Lord Rosse resolve this object into excessively minute stars, and shew filaments of stars adhering to its edges." When this nebula was unresolved, and had the character of a ring nebula, which might be produced by the rapid motion of a nebular sphere round its axis, the star dust philosopher would have considered its form as a proof that it could not consist of stars; but now that it has been resolved, we are entitled to conclude that in nebulæ, such as the spiral ones, where there is the appearance of motion, the spirals are not purely nebulous matter thrown off from the nucleus like water twirled from a mop, or by any spiral movement whatever.

As the appearance of motion, therefore, in particular nebulæ, is no proof that they consist of purely nebulous matter composed of invisible particles, we are entitled to draw the conclusion that this large class of celestial bodies are clusters of stars at an immense distance from our own system,—that each of the stars of which they are composed is the sun or centre of a system of planets, and that these planets are inhabited, or if we follow a strict analogy, that at least *one planet* in each of these numberless systems, is like our earth, the seat of vegetable, animal, and intellectual life.

Before we quit the subject of nebulæ, and purely nebulous matter, we must notice two points connected with the optical appearance of nebulæ, which we think are strong arguments in favour of their being resolvable into stars. If a nebula consisted of phosphorescent or self-luminous atoms of nebulous matter, its light would be immensely inferior in brightness to that of the same nebula composed of suns which are provided with a luminous atmosphere for the very purpose of discharging a brilliant light. When we see, therefore, two nebulæ of the very same brightness, and find by the telescope that one of them only is resolvable into stars, we can scarcely doubt that the other is similarly composed. We cannot conceive that a nebula of phosphorescent stars could be visible at such enormous distances from our system. When a planetary nebula is equally bright in every part of its disc, like that which is a little to the south of *β Ursæ Majoris*, and which resembles a *flat disc*, "presented to us in a plane precisely perpendicular to the visual ray," it is impossible to regard it as nebulous matter in a state of aggregation. In like manner, all those nebulæ, which have strange and irregular shapes, indicate the absence of any force of aggregation, and authorize us to regard them as clusters of stars.

CHAPTER X.

GENERAL SUMMARY.

The arguments for a plurality of worlds, contained in the preceding chapters, are so various, and have such different degrees of force, that different views of the subject will be taken by persons who thoroughly believe in the general doctrine. We can easily conceive why some persons may believe that all the planets which have satellites are inhabited, while they deny the inhabitability of those that have none, and also of the Sun and the satellites themselves. There are individuals, too, though we doubt their faith in sidereal astronomy, who readily believe that the whole of our planetary system is the seat of life, while they are startled by the statement that every star in the heavens, and every point in a nebula which the most powerful telescope has not separated from its neighbour, is a sun surrounded by inhabited planets like our own; and that immortal beings are swarming through universal space more numerous than drops of water in the ocean, or the grains of sand upon its shores. But if these persons really believe in the distances and magnitudes of the stars, and of the laws which govern the binary systems of double stars, they must find it equally, if not more difficult to comprehend, why innumerable suns and worlds fill the immensity of the universe, revolving round one another, and discharging their light and heat into space, without a plant to spring under their influence, without an animal to rejoice in their genial beams, and without the eye of reason to lift itself devoutly to its Creator. In peopling such worlds with life and intelligence, we *assign the cause of their existence*; and when the mind is once alive to this great truth, it cannot fail to realize the grand combination of *infinity of life with infinity of matter.*

In support of these views, we have already alluded to the almost incredible fact, that there are in our own globe hills and strata miles in length, composed of the fossil remains of microscopic insects; and we need scarcely remind the least informed of our readers, that the air which they breathe, the water which they drink, the food which they eat, the earth on which they tread, the ocean which encircles them, and the atmosphere above their heads, are swarming with universal life. Wherever we have seen matter we have seen life. Life was not made for matter, but matter for life; and in whatever spot we see its atoms, whether at our feet, or in the planets, or in the remotest star, we may be sure that life is there—life to enjoy the light and heat of God's bounty—to study His works, to recognise His glory, and to bless His name.

Those ungenial minds that can be brought to believe that the Earth is the only inhabited body in the universe, will have no difficulty in conceiving that it also might have been without inhabitants. Nay, if such minds are imbued with geological truth, they must admit that for millions of years the Earth was without inhabitants; and hence we are led to the extraordinary result, that *for millions of years there was not an intelligent creature in the vast do-*

minions of the universal King; and that before the formation of the protozoic strata, there was neither a plant nor an animal throughout the infinity of space! During this long period of universal death, when Nature herself was asleep, the Sun with his magnificent attendants, the planets with their faithful satellites, the stars in the binary systems, the Solar system itself, were performing their daily, their annual, and their secular movements, unseen, unheeded, and fulfilling no purpose that human reason can conceive,—lamps lighting nothing,—fires heating nothing,—waters quenching nothing,—clouds screening nothing,—breezes fanning nothing,—and every thing around, mountain and valley, hill and dale, earth and ocean, all *meaning nothing.*

> . . . . The Stars
> Did wander darkling in the eternal space.

To our apprehension, such a condition of the Earth, of the Solar system, and of the sidereal universe, would be the same as that of our own globe, if all its vessels of war and of commerce were traversing its seas, with empty cabins and freightless holds,—as if all the railways on its surface were in full activity without passengers and goods,—and all our machinery beating the air and gnashing their iron teeth without work performed. A house without tenants, a city without citizens, present to our minds the same idea as a planet without life, and a universe without inhabitants. Why the house was built, why the city was founded, why the planet was made, and why the universe was created, it would be difficult even to conjecture. Equally great would be the difficulty were the planets shapeless lumps of matter poised in ether, and still and motionless as the grave: But when we consider them as chiselled spheres teeming with inorganic beauty, and in full mechanical activity, performing their appointed motions with such miraculous precision, that their days and their years never err a second of time in hundreds of centuries, the difficulty of believing them to be without life is, if possible, immeasurably increased. To conceive any one material globe, whether a gigantic clod slumbering in space, or a noble planet equipped like our own, and duly performing its appointed task, to have no living occupants, or not in a state of preparation to receive them, seems to us one of those notions which could be harboured only in an ill-educated and ill-regulated mind,—a mind without faith and without hope: But to conceive a whole universe of moving and revolving worlds in such a category, indicates, in our apprehension, a mind dead to feeling and shorn of reason.

But we have been mistaken in thinking that the universe was dead: It was but unborn, the perfect chrysalis from which the living butterfly was to spring. Protozoic forms arose at the Divine command,—the infant plant, the simple mollusc, the nobler fish, the still nobler quadruped, successively appeared, and Man, the image of his Maker, and the work of His hand, was invested with the sovereignty of the globe. The Earth, therefore, was made for man, matter for life; and wherever another earth is seen, we are forced to the conviction that it was made like ours for the use of an intellectual race.

Although we have repeatedly alluded, in the preceding pages, to the absurdity of supposing suns and planets to be made without any conceivable object, yet the argument may be presented in a more general form. In all the works which are the result of human skill, the great object is to produce a given effect by the smallest expenditure of labour and of materials. The genius of the artist is less strikingly shewn in producing a new effect, than in producing one well known, with economy of time, of work, and of material. Every thing that is not necessary to the final effect of a process, or of a machine, is labour in vain,—a species of work in which man never willingly indulges. Even where labour is not hallowed by the sweat of the brow,—where it does not earn bread, or is not exhausted in the great structures of civilisation, it is never *labour in vain.* Every act of the mind, and every motion of the hand which it guides, is a step in the great march of social progress, however frivolous its work may seem, and however useless its immediate result. The toy for the child, the telescope for the sage, the locomotive for the railway, the steam-ship for the ocean, are equally, though in different degrees, the result of useful occupation. In the world of instinct there is the same economy of skill and labour,—the spider and the bee, the ant and the beaver, are spendthrifts neither of time nor of toil; and in all the works of the Divine artist around us,—in all the laws of matter and of motion,—in the frame of man and of animals, of plants and of inorganic nature, the economy of power is universally displayed. *Nothing is made in vain,—nothing by a complex process which can be made by a simple one;* and it has often been remarked by the most diligent students of the living world, that the infinite wisdom of the Creator is more strikingly displayed in the economy than in the manifestation of power.

With such truths before us, is it possible to believe that, with the exception of our little planet, all the other planets of the system, all the hundreds of comets, all the systems of the universe, *are to our reason made in vain?* It is doubtless possible that the almighty Architect of the universe may have had other objects in view, incomprehensible by us, than that of supporting animal and vegetable life in these magnificent spheres; but as the question we are discussing is one in which we can appeal only to human reason, and as human reason in its highest form cannot discover these other objects, we the inhabitants of one of the least of these spheres, which has for immeasurable periods of time been preparing for the residence of man, must believe, under the guidance of that reason, that they were destined *certainly*, like our Earth, for an intellectual race, and destined *probably* for a previous and lengthened occupation by plants and animals, in order that their inhabitants may study on the tombstones of the past those miraculous processes of growth and decay, of destruction and renovation, by which there has been provided for them so noble an inheritance.

In the celebrated sermon *On the Origin and Frame of the World*, to which we have already referred, Dr. Bentley has taken a view of this part of the question which, though slightly different from ours, leads him to the same conclusion. Considering " that the soul of one virtuous and religious man is of greater worth and excellency than the Sun and his planets, and all the stars in the world," Dr. Bentley expresses his willingness to believe, that " their usefulness to man might be the sole end of their creation, if it could be proved that they were as beneficial to" us as the Polar Star was formerly for navigation, or as the Moon is for producing the tides, and lighting us in winter nights. "But," he adds, "we dare not undertake to shew what advantage is brought to us by those innumerable stars in the galaxy and other parts of the firmament, not discernible by naked eyes, and yet each many thousand times bigger than the whole body of the Earth. If you say, they beget in us a great idea and veneration of the mighty Author and Governor of such stupendous bodies, and excite and elevate our minds to His adoration and praise; you say very truly and well. But would it not raise in us a higher apprehension of the infinite majesty and boundless beneficence of God, to suppose that these remote and vast bodies were formed not merely upon our account to be peeped at through an optic glass, but for different ends and nobler purposes? And yet who will deny but there are great multitudes of lucid stars even beyond the reach of the best telescopes; and that every visible star may have *opaque planets*[1] revolving about them which we cannot discover? Now, if they were not created for our sakes, it is certain and evident that they were not made for their own; for matter has no life nor perception, is not conscious of its own existence, nor capable of happiness, nor gives the sacrifice of praise and worship to the Author of its being. It remains, therefore, that all bodies were formed for the sake of intelligent minds: and as the Earth was principally designed for the being and service and contemplation of men; why may not all other planets be created for the like uses, each for their own inhabitants which have life and understanding?"[2]

Various attempts have been made, but without much success, to give a popular illus-

[1] This is the earliest allusion, we remember, to *dark* bodies in the sidereal regions, unless Dr. Bentley uses the word *opaque* in contradistinction to *self-luminous* bodies. The planets in single or binary systems are invisible from their distance, not from their being unable to reflect light. Mr. Pigot had long ago concluded, from various celestial phenomena, that there are "primary invisible bodies or unenlightened stars that have ever remained in eternal darkness." The late Professor Bessel having found that the proper motions of *Sirius* and *Procyon* deviate very sensibly from uniformity, has come to the conclusion, that they describe orbits in space under the influence of central forces round *dark* or *non-luminous* central bodies, not very remote from the stars themselves.

[2] Eighth Sermon, pp. 5, 6.

tration of the argument from analogy, by which we infer the existence of inhabitants in the planets, from their similarity to the Earth. M. Fontenelle, the first person who attempted this, gave the following illustration :—

"Suppose," says he, "that there never had been any communication between Paris and St. Denis, and that a person who had never been out of the city was upon the towers of Notre Dame, and saw St. Denis at a distance: He is asked if he believes that St. Denis is inhabited, like Paris. He will boldly answer, No. For he will say, I see distinctly the inhabitants of Paris; but those of St. Denis I do not see; and I never heard anybody speak of them. It is true, some will tell him, that from the towers of Notre Dame he cannot see the inhabitants of St. Denis, on account of the distance;—that all that he can see of St. Denis greatly resembles Paris;—that St. Denis has steeples, houses, and walls, and that it may very well resemble Paris in being inhabited. All this will produce no effect upon my Parisian; he will persist in maintaining that St. Denis is not inhabited, as he sees nobody.

Our St. Denis is the Moon, and each of us is this citizen of Paris, who was never out of it. You are too severe, said the Marchioness ; we are not such fools as your citizen ; for, as he sees that St. Denis is just like Paris, he must have lost his reason, if he does not believe that it is inhabited ; but the Moon is not at all made like the Earth. Take care, madam, I replied ; for if the Moon in every respect resembles the Earth, you will be obliged to believe that the Moon is inhabited."[1]

This illustration is certainly defective ; for, as Fontenelle subsequently remarks, the Moon does not so much resemble the Earth as St. Denis does Paris. The mistake which the author commits arises from his not comparing the Earth with a planet, like Jupiter, with satellites, and clouds, and trade winds, and a diurnal motion. In this case, the citizen should have been a villager looking at Paris from the steeple of St. Denis, and his answer should have been, I think it very probable that there are or have been inhabitants in Paris, but it is possible that they may have all

[1] *Œuvres de Fontenelle*, 2de Series, vol. ii. p. 49, edit. 1758.

left it, or have not yet arrived. It is just possible, too, that these walls may never have been a protection to inhabitants, nor these churches thronged, nor these houses occupied; but if this were the case, the sovereign who founded the city, who encircled it with a wall, who erected the churches, and who built the houses, must have been a fool or a madman.

A very different illustration is given by Huygens: "If any person," says he, "were shewn, in the body of a dissected dog, the heart, the stomach, the lungs, the intestines, and then the veins, the arteries, and the nerves, then, though he never saw the open body of an animal, he could hardly doubt that the same structure and variety of parts existed in the ox, the sow, and other animals. In like manner, if we knew the nature of one of the satellites of Jupiter and Saturn, would we not believe that the very same things which were found in it would be found in all the other satellites? In like manner, if we saw anything in one comet, we would conclude that this was the structure of all. There is therefore much weight in conclusions drawn from analogies, and in inferences from things that are seen to things that are not seen."[1]

The author of the Essay against a Plurality of Worlds, considers the illustration of Fontenelle as unfair; and he gives the following modification of it as representing his own argument more fairly:—

"Let it be supposed," he says, "that we inhabit an island, from which innumerable other islands are visible, but the art of navigation being quite unknown, we are ignorant whether any of them are inhabited. In some of these islands are seen masses more or less resembling churches, and some of our neighbours assert that these are churches; that churches must be surrounded by houses, and that houses must have inhabitants; others hold that the seeming churches are only peculiar forms of rocks: in this state of the debate everything depends upon the degree of resemblance to churches which the forms exhibit. But suppose that telescopes are invented and employed with diligence on the questionable shapes. In a long course of careful and skilful examination, no house is seen, and

[1] *Cosmotheoros*, &c., lib. i. Hugenii *Opera*, tom. ii. pp. 652, 653.

the rocks do not at all become more like churches, rather the contrary. So far, it would seem, the probability of inhabitants in the islands is lessened. But there are other reasons brought into view. Our island is a long extinct volcano, with a tranquil and fertile soil, but the other islands are apparently somewhat different. Some of them are active volcanoes, the volcanic operations covering, so far as we can discern, the whole island ; others undergo changes, such as weather or earthquakes may produce ; but in none of them can we discover such changes as shew the hand of man. For these islands, it would seem, the probability of inhabitants is further lessened.[1] And so long as we have no better evidence than these for forming a judgment, it would surely be accounted rash to assert that the islands in general are inhabited ; and unreasonable to blame those who deny or doubt it. Nor would such blame be justified by adducing theological or *a priori* arguments ; as that the analogy of islands with islands makes the assumption allowable ; or that it is inconsistent

[1] The observation of volcanoes and church-like rocks, by the telescope, has no parallel in the analogy of the planets. It is not the moon that our author is dealing with, but innumerable planets.

with the plan of the Creator of islands to leave them uninhabited. For we know that many islands are or were long uninhabited. And if ours were an island occupied by a numerous, well-governed, moral, and religious race, of which the history was known, and of which the relation to the Creator was connected with its history; the assumption of a history, more or less similar to ours, for the inhabitants of the other islands, whose existence was utterly unproved, would, probably, be generally deemed a fitter field for the romance writer than for the philosopher. It could not, at best, rise above the region of vague conjecture."[1]

This illustration is, we think, so unfair, and so constructed to answer the author's purpose, that we concur in his opinion that the probability of the islands being inhabited "does not rise above the region of vague conjecture." No illustration indeed can be fair or effective, unless it relates to *separate* and *independent* works of God, from the condition of one of which we draw inferences by analogy relative to the state of others of which we know nothing, excepting their points

[1] *Of the Plurality of Worlds,* An Essay, pp. 157-159.

of similitude. In the illustration of Huygens, for example, the dog, the ox, and the sow, are independent existences, of whose internal structure we know nothing ; but having found certain organs upon dissecting the dog, we infer the existence of the same organs in the ox, from the external similitude in their general form, and in various external parts. In the parallel between islands and planets, the peopled islands should have been invested with certain properties or conditions necessary for its inhabitants, which should have been possessed by the other islands. The inhabited island too, should have been made as small in reference to the rest as the Earth is to Jupiter and Saturn. But independent of these defects in the illustration, the mind of the reader is otherwise prepared to admit that they may have no inhabitants, because we know of hundreds of islands without inhabitants. We can assign also a very good reason why they were made, and why they are not inhabited, and if we were to be assured of the fact, it would excite no surprise whatever. We could not say that God therefore made them in vain, because when the art of navigation is discovered, they may be found to contain gold and silver, coal and iron, and excellent harbours, such as exist in our inhabited island. We, the islanders, may suppose also, that the islands either have been or will be inhabited, and we are entitled to make this supposition, because we must have been originally created upon it, and not brought there by the art of navigation; and consequently the same creation of inhabitants may have taken place, or may yet take place, in the uninhabited ones. It is obvious, from these remarks, that the previous knowledge of the reader, to whom the appeal is made, influences what he conceives would be the speculation of the islander; and the confusion of ideas which thus takes place, renders the illustration illusory.

The best illustration which we can conceive, is to suppose a philosopher contemplating from a distance the bodies of the Solar system, and wholly ignorant of their condition. He examines them so as to acquire all the knowledge which we possess of their size—their motions—the influences they receive from the sun, and all the phenomena disclosed by the telescope. He knows nothing about their being inhabited or uninhabited, but being permitted to visit the Earth, he finds it inhabited, and observes the relation which exists between vegetable, animal, and intellectual life,—the influences which emanate from the sun and moon, and the days and nights, and seasons and atmospheric changes which characterize our globe. He then takes his place in the distance, and pondering over all the bodies of the system, he will doubtless conclude that they are all inhabited like the Earth. Had he first visited Jupiter, with its gorgeous magnitude and numerous satellites, and found it inhabited, he might have conceived it *possible* that as the monarch of the system, it might alone have enjoyed the dignity of being the seat of life ; but even in this case, the force of analogy would have compelled him to view the Solar system as one great material scheme planned by its Creator, as the residence of moral and intellectual life.

CHAPTER XI.

REPLY TO OBJECTIONS DRAWN FROM GEOLOGY.

In the preceding chapters we have submitted to the reader the facts and arguments by which the doctrine of a plurality of worlds may be maintained, and we have, at the same time, endeavoured to answer a variety of objections of a moral and scientific nature, which naturally presented themselves in discussions involving so many considerations. We have now, however, a more arduous duty to perform. The author of the Essay to which we have frequently had occasion to refer, has devoted a whole volume to an elaborate attack upon the doctrine we have been supporting. With acquirements of the highest order, and talents of no common kind, which, we think, might have been more usefully employed, he has marshalled all the truths and theories of geology, and all the facts of astronomy, against popular and deeply cherished opinions—opinions which the humblest Christian has shared with the most distinguished philosophers and divines, and which no interests, moral or religious, require us to surrender. In questions of doubtful speculation with which vulgar error is largely mingled, we applaud the writer who boldly girds himself for the task of exposing presumption and ignorance, however generally they may prevail ; but in the case with which we are dealing, where the opinions assailed are entrenched in right feeling and embalmed in the warmth of the affections, and where they are as probable as the theories and speculations by which they are to be superseded, we can ascribe to no better feeling than a love of notoriety any attempt to ridicule or unsettle them.

The first and the most plausible of the arguments maintained by the Essayist is drawn from geological facts and theories. We have already, in a preceding chapter, explained these facts, and admitted, with certain limitations, (which, to give our opponent every advantage, we at present abandon,) that during a long period of time when the Earth was preparing for the residence of man, it was the seat only of vegetable and animal life.

Since the Earth, then, was during a very long time (a *million*[1] of years we shall say) uninhabited by intelligent beings, our author draws the conclusion that all the *other planets may be occupied at present with a life no higher than that of the brutes, or with no life at all;* that is, that there is not a plurality of worlds inhabited by rational beings. Now this is not the conclusion which the premises authorize. If God took a million of years to prepare the Earth for man, the probability is, that all the planets were similarly prepared for inhabitants, and that they are *now* occupied by rational beings. If one or more of them are only in the act of being prepared, and are not yet the seat of intelligence, analogy forces us to the conclusion, that they will be inhabited like the Earth. The assertion that they may be occupied by *no life at all,* is contrary to all analogy, unless we

[1] We use this number to avoid circumlocution. The Essayist uses the word *myriads* of years, as the period of only one of the earliest formations!

suppose that all the planets are only in that stage of preparation which preceded the *protozoic* age,—a supposition which no person is entitled to make, but which, if it were true, would prove that the time was approaching when all the planets were to be inhabited, like the Earth.

It is admitted by every geologist that the Earth was not only made to be a fit residence for the human family, but that it was made in such a manner that man might see the wonderful processes by which it was prepared, and read its vast chronology in the history of its fossil remains. Is it not probable, therefore, that the other planets were formed in a similar manner, and with a similar object? And if analogy leads us to believe that all the planets have been or are in the *azoic*, or *protozoic*, or *palæozoic* stage of formation, the conclusion is inevitable, that they are occupied, or are about to be occupied, by beings formed after God's image; and consequently, that there is a plurality of worlds. We may put the argument in a simpler form. In the time of Huygens and Fontenelle and Bentley, when the Mosaic account of the creation was adopted in its literal meaning, the argument from analogy had a certain degree of force. Has that degree of force been diminished by the subsequent discovery that a million of years, in place of six days, were occupied in the preparation of the Earth ? The argument from analogy is not only not affected by this discovery, but the discovery itself furnishes us with the new ground of analogy, that planets are made for the very purpose of being inhabited,—that they are made in such a way as to teach their inhabitants the wonderful processes by which the Almighty has made them,—and that they are made of materials essentially necessary for man's personal and social happiness. Man was not made for the planet—but the planet was made for man.

Quitting the ground of analogy, our author has recourse to what we consider the most ingenious, though shallow, piece of sophistry which we have ever encountered in modern dialectics. He founds an elaborate argument on the mutual relation of an *atom of time* and an *atom of space*, comparing the different periods of time occupied in the formation of the Earth with the different distances in space. In this process, he divides the great geological period into *four* periods of *time*, and the infinity of space into *four* lengths of space; and he "assumes that the numbers which express the antiquity of the four periods" are "on the same scale as the numbers which express the *four* magnitudes," or lengths of space. We have placed these periods in contrast in the following table, to exhibit clearly the nature of the argument:—

TIME.	SPACE.
1. "The *Present* organic condition of the Earth."	1. "The magnitude of the *Earth*."
2. "The *Tertiary* period of geologists which preceded that."	2. "The magnitude of the Solar system compared with the Earth."
3. "The *Secondary* period which was anterior to that."	3. "The distance of the nearest *fixed stars* compared with the *Solar system*."
4. "The *Primary* period which preceded the Secondary."	4. "The distance of the *most remote nebulæ* compared with the *nearest fixed star*."

In this table of *Time* and *Space*, the time during which the Earth has been in its present condition, which is nearly 6000 years, is contrasted with the magnitude of the Earth, which is 8000 miles nearly in diameter, and these numbers are units in the scale, the one being called an *atom of time* compared with the duration of the primary geological period, and the other an *atom of space* compared with the distance of the remotest nebulæ. Now the importance, or the *significance* of the Earth, in regard to space, is fairly measured by its diameter of 8000 miles, which is a fixed quantity; but its significance with regard to time is not measured by 6000 years, because its duration is constantly increasing, and every year adds to its *significance;* that is, the *atom of time* is approximating to infinity, while the atom of space is invariable. Admitting, however, our author's premises, let us consider his extraordinary conclusions:—

"We find," says he, "*that man* (the human race, from its present origin till now) *has occupied but an atom of time*, as he *has occupied but an atom of space.*" And again,—

"The scale of man's *insignificance* is of the same order in reference to *time* as to *space.* . . . . If the Earth as the habitation of man is a *speck* in the midst of an infinity of space, the Earth as the habitation of man is also a *speck* at the end of an infinity of time. If we are as *nothing* in the surrounding universe, we are as *nothing* in the elapsed eternity; or rather in the elapsed organic antiquity during which the Earth has existed, and been the abode of life. . . . . Or, is the objection this? That if we suppose the Earth only to be occupied with inhabitants, all the other objects of the universe are *waste*, turned to no purpose? Is *work* of this kind unsuited to the character of the Creator? But here, again, *we have the like waste* in the occupation of the Earth. *All its previous ages have been wasted upon mere brute life*; after, so far as we can see, for myriads of years upon the lowest, the least conscious forms of life, upon shell-fish, corals, sponges. Why, then, should not the seas and continents of other planets *be occupied at present with a life no higher than this*, OR WITH NO LIFE AT ALL. . . . The intelligent part of creation is *thrust* into the *compass of a few years* in the course of myriads of ages; why then not into the *compass of a few miles* in the expanse of systems? . . . . If then the Earth be the sole inhabited spot in the work of creation, the oasis in the desert of our system, there is nothing in this contrary to the analogy of creation."

That is, *The Earth, the* ATOM OF SPACE, *is the only one of the planetary and sidereal worlds that is inhabited, because it was so long without inhabitants, and has been occupied only an* ATOM OF TIME! If any of our readers see the force of this argument, they must possess an acuteness of perception to which we lay no claim. To us it is not only illogical;—it is a mere sound in the ear, without any sense in the brain. What relation is there between *the* SHORT *period of man's occupation of the Earth,* and *the* SMALL *portion which he occupies in space?* If there is such a relation, that we can reason from the truth of the *first* to the probability of the *second,* then we can reason as justly from the truth of the *second* to the probability of the *first.* Now, let us suppose it to be as certain that the Earth is the only inhabited planet, as it is certain that Man has occupied the Earth only for the short period of 6000 years, could any rational being allege that because man occupied only an atom of space, he therefore must live only an atom of time upon the Earth?

But even if we admit the result with regard to Man, the argument does not apply to other intellectual beings than Man—to an inferior or to a superior race that never occupied the Earth at all. If man is thus limited by a syllogism to the occupation of one planet, one atom of space,—an angelic race, who never lived on the Earth at all, may be indulged with the occupation of Jupiter. But, farther, let us suppose that we learn by the telescope that every planet and satellite in the Solar system is inhabited by *Man*, he would still occupy but an *atom of space*, and our author's argument would go to prove that none of the fixed stars or binary systems are inhabited. In like manner, if we could prove that the binary systems were inhabited, the sum of them all would be but an atom of space, and our author would still rejoice in his conclusion, that the clusters of stars and nebulæ were uninhabited vapour.

If the reasoning which we have examined be sound in its nature, it would fail entirely by a change in the premises. If it is *possible*, that the time of the Earth's preparation was comparatively short, or that intelligent beings occupied the Earth previous to man ; and if it is *probable* that Man will continue to occupy the Earth during a period equal, or approximating to the period of the Earth's preparation, the whole of our author's argument has neither force nor meaning.

If the Almighty has occupied a million of years in preparing the crust of the Earth as a suitable residence for man, by the slow operation of secondary causes, and has deposited the remains of vegetable and animal life in each series of its formation, in order to enable man to read the history of his omnipotence and wisdom, is that any reason why the Earth, the residence of man, should, among countless and more glorious worlds than his own, be *the only one that is inhabited?* Reason and common sense dictate a very different opinion. If *nearly infinity of time* has been employed to provide for intellectual and immortal life so glorious an abode, is it not probable that *nearly infinity* of space will be devoted to the same noble purpose ?

CHAPTER XII.

OBJECTIONS FROM THE NATURE OF NEBULÆ.

In a preceding chapter on nebulæ, we trust we have satisfied the candid inquirer that all nebulæ are clusters of stars, and that there is no proof whatever, not even the shadow of proof, that in the sidereal regions there is what is called nebulous matter, either existing in a stationary condition, or aggregating into stars. The author of the Essay *Of the Plurality of Worlds*, whose astronomical objections to the doctrine of a plurality of worlds we are about to consider, very dexterously commences his argument with an attack upon that part of the doctrine which relates to nebulæ. He is not content with the statement of facts, but he attempts to throw ridicule upon his opponents by the application of words which are calculated to influence the minds of ignorant or inattentive readers. By calling nebulæ *clouds*, and pieces of *comets' tails*, and the stars into which they are resolved, *shining dots*, pieces of bright *curd*, luminous *grains*, and *lumps of light*, he fancies that he has demolished the opinion of astronomers that these *dots* are suns; that they are "as far from each other as the dog-star" is from us; that each sun has its system of planets, and each planet its animal and vegetable life.

"An astronomer," says the Essayist, "armed with a powerful telescope, *resolves* a nebula, discerns that a luminous cloud is composed of shining dots:—but what are these dots? Into what does he resolve the nebula? Into *stars*, it is commonly said. Let us not wrangle about words. By all means let these dots be stars, if we know about what we are speaking,—if a *star* merely means a luminous dot in the sky. But that these stars shall resemble in their nature stars of the first magnitude, and that such stars shall resemble our sun, are surely very bold structures of assumption to build on such a basis. Some nebulæ are resolvable—are resolvable into distinct points—certainly a very curious, probably a very important discovery. We may hereafter learn, that *all* nebulæ are resolvable into distinct points; that would be a still more curious discovery. But what would it amount to? What would be the simple way of expressing it without hypothesis and without assumption? Plainly this,—that the substance of all nebulæ is not continuous but discrete;—separable and separate into distinct luminous elements; nebulæ are, it would thus seem, as it were, of a *curdled* or *granulated* texture; they have run into *lumps of light*, or have been formed originally of such lumps. Highly curious! But what are these lumps? How large are they? At what distances? Of what structure? Of what use? It would seem that he must be a bold man who undertakes to answer these questions. Certainly he must appear to *ordinary thinkers* to be *very* bold, who, in reply, says gravely and confidently, as if he had authority for his teaching, These lumps, O man, are suns; they are distant from each other as far as the dog-star is from us; each has its system of planets, which revolve around it; and each of these planets is the seat of an animal and vegetable creation. Among these planets some, we do not yet know how many, are occupied by rational and responsible creatures like man ; and the only matter which perplexes us, holding this belief on astronomical grounds, is, that we do not quite see how to put our theology into its due place and form in our system."[1]

This, surely, is neither the language nor the tone of a man of science in search of truth, or holding in respect the great revelations of astronomy. The Essayist triumphantly asks *four* questions, and tells us that he would be a *bold* man that undertakes to answer them. We accept the challenge, and appeal to our readers.

Question 1. *How large are the lumps of light*, or the shining dots, into which the astronomer's powerful telescope has resolved the nebulæ? These lumps of light are admitted to be *stars* shining by their own light. Now, it has been shewn by the most distinguished astronomers, by Herschel and by Struve, that in the various order of distances in space, the distances of the nebulæ are the greatest. According to the recent researches of Mr. Peters, as given by M.

[1] *Essay*, pp. 120-122.

Struve,[1] the following are the distances of the stars of different magnitudes, as ascertained by a process approximately correct:—

Apparent Magnitudes.	Parallaxes.	Distances in radii of Earth's orbit.
1, . .	0″·209	98600
2, . .	0″·116	1778000
3, . .	0″·076	2725000
4, . .	0″·054	3850000
5, . .	0″·037	5378000
6, . .	0″·027	7616000
8½, . .	0″·008	24490000
11½, . .	0″·00092	224500000

As the nebulæ are obviously more remote than any of the stars in the above table, and as the nearest of these stars must, from their distance, be equal to our sun, we are entitled to conclude, that the stars or nebulæ must be of a much greater size. Sir John Herschel observes, that "when we consider that the united lustre of a group or *globular* cluster of stars, affects the eye with a less impression of light than a star of the *fourth* magnitude, (for the largest of these clusters is scarcely visible to the naked eye,) the idea *we are thus compelled to form* of their distance from us may prepare us *for almost any*

[1] *Etudes d'Astronomie Stellaire.*

estimate of their dimensions. A visible *dot*, or a visible *lump*, must therefore be a body of enormous magnitude, and though we cannot give its size in miles or diameters of the Earth, we are sure that every astronomer in the old or the new world will allow that we have answered the question with sufficient accuracy in reference to the object for which it was asked. *The size of the* DOT *or lump is of sufficient magnitude to be a sun.*

Quest. 2. *At what distances* are the dots or lumps from one another?

In order to answer this question, the Essayist knows well that we require to have the apparent distance between the centres of the *dots*, and upon the supposition that the two dots are at the same distance from us, we can easily determine their distance from the parallax which may be assumed for resolvable nebulæ. There are double stars in the binary system, whseo apparent distance is as small as that of the *dots* or stars in the nebulæ, and yet every astronomer admits that between them, there is ample room for a system of planets round each.

Quest. 3. *What is the structure* of these dots

or stars? The author certainly does not expect to learn whether these are made of *granite* or *greywacke.* Analogy teaches us that their structure will be similar to that of the only sun with which we are acquainted. It will consist of a luminous envelope enclosing a dark nucleus.

Quest. 4. *What is the use of the dots or stars?* Being large bodies, and self-luminous, they can be of no conceivable use but to give light to planets, or to the solid nuclei of which they consist.

Having thus given answers to our author's questions,—answers which we are confident would be given by every astronomer, may we not ask in return,—What is the *size*, and *distance*, and *structure*, and *use* of the dots upon his hypothesis, that they are patches of comets' tails or luminous *grains?* The Essayist is silent. Should he be the *very bold man* to make the attempt, the astronomical world would repudiate his theory and his answers.

But there is another way of meeting objections of such an unreasonable character. Our author is a firm believer in the geological speculation, that the Earth required "*myriads of millions*" of years for its formation, and assuming his principle of contrasting time and space, may we not ask him in return, What was the structure of the primitive Earth? What were the periods of time required for the deposition of each formation? And of what use was an arrangement requiring *myriads of millions of years* for its completion?

Believing that "nebulæ are vast masses of incoherent, or gaseous matter, of immense tenuity, and destitute of solid moving bodies," a theory which he derives from another theory called the *nebular hypothesis*, without adducing the least trace of evidence in its support, our author boasts, not surely in the spirit of the inductive philosophy, that *he seems to have made it* CERTAIN that the *celestial objects* (the nebulæ) *are not inhabited.* To this we reply, that we have made it MORE PROBABLE that the CELESTIAL *objects are inhabited,*—an assertion less presumptuous, but more certain than his.

We have described in a preceding chapter the *spiral nebulæ* discovered by Lord Rosse, and we have endeavoured to explain the appearance of motion, which may be considered as indicated by the spirals which they exhibit. With his accustomed boldness, and extravagance of speculation, our Essayist has made the following observations on these spiral forms: —" The comet of Encke," he affirms, " describes a spiral gradually converging to the Sun," and " in 30,000 years this comet *will* complete its spiral, and be absorbed in the central mass. . . . . . But this spiral converging to its pole so slowly that it reaches it only after forming 10,000 circuits (or spirals,") while " there are at most three or more circular or oval sweeps in each spiral (of the nebulæ), or even the spiral reaches the centre before it has completed a single revolution round it." From data like these, the following theory of the spiral nebulæ is deduced:—" If we suppose the comet (that of Encke) to consist of a luminous mass, *or a string of masses*, which would occupy a considerable arch of such an orbit, the orbit would be marked by a track of light as an oval spiral, or if such a comet were to separate into two portions, as *we have, with our own eyes, recently seen Biela's Comet do*, or into a greater number; then these portions would be distributed along such a spiral. And if we suppose a large mass of cometic matter thus to move in a highly resisting medium, and to consist of patches of different densities, then some would move faster, and some more slowly, but all in spirals, such as have been spoken of, and the general aspect produced would be that of the *Spiral Nebulæ*, which I have endeavoured to describe." A hypothesis more wild and gratuitous than this was never before submitted to the scientific world. In what part of the nebula do the cometic patches reside before they begin their motion of descent to the nucleus; and what is the cause of their quitting their place of rest? No comet out of the many hundreds that have been observed, has been so negligent of its tail as to leave it behind. Encke's Comet has been equally careful of its appendage, and the division of Biela's Comet was only *apparent*. But even if a comet were to separate into a number of portions, these portions would, like the division of Biela's Comet, travel along with it and again unite themselves into one, so that the analogy of this comet is destructive of the speculation which it is brought to support.

CHAPTER XIII.

OBJECTIONS FROM THE NATURE OF THE FIXED STARS AND BINARY SYSTEMS.

HAVING, as our author congratulates himself, "cleared away the supposed inhabitants from the outskirts of creation, so far as the nebulæ are the outskirts of creation," he proceeds to consider the fixed stars, and examine any evidence which he may be able to discover as to the probability of their containing in themselves, or in their accompanying bodies, as planets, inhabitants of any kind. We have already stated the grounds upon which the most distinguished astronomers have believed that single and double stars are accompanied with planets similar to our own; and we shall now consider the objections which are made to this opinion.

Beginning with *clusters of stars*, the author whose opinions we have been controverting, justly observes, that they are in the same category with resolvable nebulæ, and he therefore regards it as "a very bold assumption to assume, without any farther proof, that these *bright points* are suns, distant from each other as far as we are from the nearest stars. When these *clusters* are *globular*, Sir John Herschel regards their form as "indicating the existence of some general bond of union in the nature of an attractive force;" and assuming that the "globular space may be filled with equal stars, uniformly dispersed through it, and very numerous, each of them attracting every other with a force inversely as the square of the distance, . . . each star would describe a perfect ellipse about the common centre of gravity as its centre," Sir John therefore conceives that "such a system might subsist, and realize in a great measure that abstract and ideal harmony which Newton has shewn to characterize a law of force directly as the distance."

Referring to this ingenious theory of globular clusters, the Essayist illustrates it by asserting, that if "our Sun were broken into fragments, so as to fill the sphere girdled by the Earth's orbit, all the fragments would revolve round the centre in a year," and as there is no symptom in any cluster of its parts moving so fast, he concludes that clusters, like nebulæ, must be extremely rare, that is, vaporous, like the tails of comets. In support of this view of the subject, he alleges that the boldness of the opposite opinion, that they are suns, *appears to be felt* by our wisest astronomer, meaning Sir John Herschel, to whom he refers in such a manner as if Sir John maintained the same opinion with himself. This, however, is far from being the case, as his own words will prove: "*Perhaps*," says he, "it may be thought to savour of the gigantesque to look upon the individuals of such a group as suns like our own, and their mutual distances as equal to those which separate our sun from the nearest fixed star: *yet*, when we consider that their united lustre affects the eye with a less impression of light than a star of the fourth magnitude, the idea *we are thus compelled* to form of their distance from us may prepare us for almost any estimate of their dimensions."[1]

The same just views of the sidereal system, in which no motion is visible, are taken by Dr. Whewell, in his Bridgewater Treatise.[2] "Astronomy," says he, "teaches us that the stars which we see have no immediate relation to our system. The *obvious supposition* is, that they are of the nature and order of our sun: the minuteness of their apparent magnitude agrees, on this supposition, with *the enormous and almost inconceivable* distance which, from all the measurements of astronomers, we are led to attribute to them. *If, then, these are suns, they may, like our sun, have planets revolving round them,* and *these* may, like our planet, be *the seats of vegetable, animal, and rational life*:—we may thus have in the universe worlds, no one knows how many, no one can guess how varied; but, however many, however varied, they are still but so many provinces in the same empire, subject to common rules, governed by a common power."

[1] *Outlines*, &c., § 866, referred to by the Essayist.
[2] Book III. chap. ii. p. 270.

From the globular clusters of stars our author proceeds to the binary systems, of which we have treated in a preceding chapter. He admits that the law of universal gravitation is established for several of these systems, "with as complete evidence as that which carries its operation to the orbits of Uranus and Neptune," but he endeavours to shew that each of the stars of the best known binary systems, *a Centauri* and 61 *Cygni*, "*may have its luminous matter diffused through a globe as large as the Earth's annual orbit*," and that, in this case, "it would not *be more* dense than the tail of a comet." It is in vain to argue against assertions like these, which can only be met by an equally positive denial of them. In the present case, however, we can do more. Sir John Herschel has shewn that the sum of the two masses of the double star 61 *Cygni*, is to that of the Sun as 0·353 to 1, or nearly as 1 to 3·1, and hence he concludes, that "the Sun is neither vastly greater nor vastly less than the stars composing 61 *Cygni*." The conclusion, therefore, of the Essayist, that the matter of these systems, "of these brilliant constituents," as

Sir John Herschel calls them, would fill the Earth's orbit, and have the rarity of comets' tails, is contrary to astronomical truth.

We have already seen that Sir John Herschel considers these double stars as suns, "accompanied with their trains of planets and satellites," and has stated the conditions necessary for the *existence of their inhabitants.* To our Essayist such a scheme appears so *complex*, that it would be "impossible to arrange it in a stable manner," so as to protect the inhabitants from *such dangers*, and he considers himself as having overturned Sir John Herschel's view, by simply asserting, without a ground even for the assertion, that "their sun may be a vast sphere of luminous matter, and the planets, plunged into this atmosphere, may, instead of describing regular orbits, plough their way in spiral paths through the nebulous abyss to its central nucleus"!

Having obtained, as our author sarcastically remarks, "but little promise of inhabitants from clustered stars and double stars," he turns his attention to the *single stars* as the most hopeful cases, and asks, "what is the probability that the fixed stars or some of them really have planets revolving round them ?" To this he justly replies, that " the only proof that the fixed stars are the centres of planetary systems, resides in the assumption that these stars are *like the sun* ;—resemble him in their qualities and nature, and therefore must have the same offices and the same appendage."

In admitting that the stars, like the sun, shine with an independent light, our author attempts to reduce the force of this point of resemblance by asserting, that " they resemble not only the sun, but nebulous patches in the sky, and the tails of comets," and that " there is no obvious distinction between the original light of the stars and the reflected light of the planets." Now these statements are either irrelevant or erroneous. The nebulous patches are clusters of stars. It is not true that comets' tails are self-luminous, and it is utterly untrue that star light and planet light are the same. Our author ought to have known that the reflected light of the planets contains precisely the same definite dark lines in their spectra as the light of the sun, which it ought to do, as it is the same light ;

while it has been proved by the direct observations of Fraunhofer and others, that the light of *Sirius*, *Procyon*, and other stars, is essentially different, having definite dark lines which do not exist in the light of the sun.

His next assertion is, that though the mass of certain stars is one-third of that of the sun, yet their matter *may be* diffused through a sphere equal to the earth's annual orbit, and that this may be the matrix, so to speak, both of the sun and planets of a system not yet formed—thus taking for granted the truth of the nebular theory, adopted by the author of the *Vestiges of Creation*, and maintained only by persons who have very erroneous ideas of creation. The worlds were not made by the operation of law, but by the immediate agency of the Almighty. Sir Isaac Newton considered the nebular theory as tending to Atheism, and in his five interesting letters to Dr. Bentley, he has ably controverted it. "The growth of new systems," he says, "out of old ones, (the doctrine maintained by the Essayist,) without the mediation of a Divine power, seems to me apparently absurd." "The diurnal rotation of the planets could not be derived from gravity, *but required a Divine* arm to impress them." "The same power," says Newton, "whether natural or supernatural, which placed the sun in the centre of the six primary planets, placed *Saturn* in the centre of the orb of his five secondary planets; and *Jupiter* in the centre of his four secondary planets; and the *Earth* in the centre of the moon's orbit; and therefore had this cause been a blind one, *without contrivance or design*, the sun would have been a body of the same kind with *Saturn*, *Jupiter*, and the *Earth*; that is *without* light or heat. Why there is one body in our system qualified to give light and heat to all the rest, I know no reason, but because the Author of the system thought it convenient: and why there is but one body of this kind, I know no reason, but because one was sufficient to warm and enlighten all the rest."[1]

That the stars undergo changes in their mechanical condition, the Essayist considers to be proved by observation. One of these proofs is the different colours of different stars, a fact certainly, but not a proof of change. Had their

[1] *Newtoni Opera*, tom. iv. pp. 430, 438.

colours changed,[1] we might have inferred a change of condition ; but knowing that no such change takes place, our author most presumptuously regards " their different colours as arising from their being at different stages of their progress," an opinion without a shadow of probability either from observation or analogy. His next proof of change is derived from the " mighty changes of which we have evidence in the view which geology gives us of the history of this Earth ;" but this is no proof at all. The changes there referred to are mere changes in the crust of the Earth, and not in its mechanical condition, and changes too, which would not show themselves even to the moon by any change of colour or of aspect. " *If,* therefore," the Essayist continues, " *stellar globes can become planetary systems* in the progress of ages, it will not be at all inconsistent with what we know of the *order of nature,* that only a few, or even that only *one,* (our Earth he means,) should have yet reached that condition. *All the others* but the

[1] Ptolemy is said to have noted Sirius as a *red* star, though it is now white. Sirius twinkles with *red* and *blue* light, and Ptolemy's eyes, like those of several other persons, may have been more sensitive to the *red* than to the *blue* rays.

one (our Earth) may be systems yet unformed, (or *fragments* or *sparks* as he subsequently calls them,) *struck off in the forming of the one!*" To such a succession of assertions and hypotheses it is scarcely necessary to reply. Stellar globes have never become planetary systems; and nature has no such order. We are thus thrown back to the astronomy of Julius Cæsar:

> "The skies are *painted* with unnumbered *sparks*."
>
> SHAKESPEARE.

The next argument adduced by our author, that the stars are unlike our sun, is the existence of changes in the stars supposed to be indicated by the disappearance of some stars, the appearance of others, and the variations in the light of a considerable number. The disappearance of a star *proves* only that it has turned a dark side to our system, and the appearance of a new star, that its luminous side has come round to us in the course of its rotation; while the variations in the light of others may arise from spots upon their surface, from eclipses by their planets, or from obscuration from comets' tails, when the variations are of an irregular character. From all these causes our own sun may be a variable star to other planets. To us even its light is diminished when large spots come across its disc; and when we consider the great number of comets which belong to our system, and the immense magnitude of their tails, the sun's light must be occasionally obscured by the interposition of these imperfectly transparent bodies.

That the Fixed Stars are *like* our sun in every point in which it is possible to compare them, will not now be doubted we think by our readers. That they are suns themselves, as Copernicus, Galileo, Kepler, and Huygens, and every astronomer believes, and as all analogy proves, is a doctrine which, we trust, will equally command their faith.

In concluding his chapter on the Fixed Stars, our Essayist utters sentiments, and throws out conjectures so insulting to Astronomy, and casting such ridicule even on the subject of his own work, that we can ascribe them only to some morbid condition of the mental powers, which feeds upon paradox, and delights in doing violence to sentiments deeply cherished, and to opinions universally believed. We almost doubt the accuracy of our vision, when we read the conjecture that the glorious stars which compose the sidereal universe,—that " Arcturus, Orion, and the Pleiades," which Scripture tells us " God made," were never created by Him at all, and " are really long since extinct !" He had previously stated, " that in consequence of the time employed in the transmission of visual impressions, our seeing a star is evidence not that it exists now, but that it existed it may be many thousands of years ago ;" and thinking that such a statement might seem to some readers to throw doubts upon reasonings which he had employed, he makes the following observation :—" It may be said that a star which was *a mere chaos* when the light by which we see it set out from it, may, in the thousands of years which have since elapsed, *have grown into an orderly world.* To which *bare possibility* we may oppose another supposition, *at least equally possible,* that *the distant stars were sparks or fragments struck off in the formation of the Solar system, which are* REALLY *long since extinct, and survive in appearance only by the light which they at first emitted"!*

With such a speculation before us, we need not put the question with which we intended to conclude this chapter. If the *stars* are not *suns*, for what conceivable purpose were they created? Our author has answered the question by asserting, that they were never created at all! To such philosophy and theology we prefer that of the poet—

> "Each of these stars is a religious house;
> I saw their altars smoke, their incense rise,
> And heard hosannahs ring through every sphere.
> The great Proprietor's all-bounteous hand
> Leaves nothing waste, but sows these fiery fields
> With seeds of reason, which to virtues rise
> Beneath his genial ray."
>
> YOUNG.

CHAPTER XIV.

OBJECTIONS FROM THE NATURE OF THE PLANETS.

HAVING sullied the glories of the sidereal world by converting the stars and systems which compose it, into vapour, gas, and comets' tails, the Essayist proceeds to apply the same process to the planets of the Solar system, converting those exterior to the Earth into *water and mud*, and the interior ones into *cinder* or *sheets of rigid slag like the moon !*

This process commences with *Neptune*, which he describes as *a dark and cold world*, where the light and heat of the Sun is incapable of "unfolding the vital powers, and cherishing the vital enjoyments of animals ;"—an assumption without any evidence to support it. It is true, that if we consider the solar influences as emanations following a geometrical law, their power upon the surface of Neptune must be immensely enfeebled; but such a law does not exist. Although the Sun is nearest the Earth in winter, his light and heat are, from different causes, greatly reduced, and we know, as we have shewn in a former chapter, that there may be conditions of the *atmosphere* of the remoter planets which may procure for them more genial influence from the Sun, or there may be temperatures in their interior which may supply the place of radiated heat.

The same observations which apply to Neptune are applicable to *Uranus*, *Saturn*, and *Jupiter*,—the same objections on the part of the Essayist, and the same reply to them. Jupiter, however, is the planet to which he especially calls our attention; and after much irrelevant speculation respecting the internal condition of our globe, as produced by the superincumbent weight of its outer formations, and "allowing for the compression of the interior parts of Jupiter," he pronounces it "tolerably certain that his density is not greater than it would be if his entire globe were composed of water," and he concludes that Jupiter must be *a mere sphere of water.* He afterwards states that there is "much evidence against the existence of solid land" in that planet; but in opposition to this evidence, he subsequently contributes *a few cinders at the centre*,—articles, doubtless, of peculiar value and interest, where everything else is water. The existence of *cinders*, however, where there is *no heat*, and where, as we shall presently see, the water is *ice*, must have perplexed his chemistry, and hence he wisely withdraws them, by telling us that the waters in Jupiter are *bottomless*, that is, *without a nucleus of cinders.*

In order to prove that *Jupiter* and the exterior planets cannot be inhabited, he adduces the *extreme* cold which must exist upon their surface; but when his assertion that Jupiter is a *sphere of water*, and, if peopled at all, peopled with *cartilaginous* and *glutinous monsters, boneless, watery, pulpy creatures*, floating in the fluid, is met with the objection that *the waters must be frozen into* ice, he has no difficulty in making Jupiter as *hot* to answer this one purpose, as he formerly made it *cold* to answer another. In this wonderful process of *adaptation*, our author's genius and his inductive method are singularly displayed. No difficulty is to him unsurmountable. In his omniscience of speculation he finds a theory for anything or everything ; " Even in the outer regions of our atmosphere," he says, " the cold is *probably* very many degrees below freezing, and in the blank and airless void beyond, it *may be* colder still. It has been calculated by physical philosophers, on grounds which seem to be solid, that the cold in the space beyond our atmosphere is 100° below Zero. *The space near to Jupiter*, IF AN ABSOLUTE VACUUM, in which there is no *matter to receive and retain*, MAY, PERHAPS, BE NO COLDER THAN IT IS NEARER THE SUN !" Were we to indulge in arbitrary conjectures like these, we could refute, without argument, all our author's objections to a plurality of worlds ; but without availing ourselves of so destructive a weapon, may we not, upon good grounds, prefer the *probable ice* to the *possible water*, and accommodate the inhabitants of Jupiter with very comfortable quarters, in huts of snow and houses of crystal, warmed by subterranean heat, and lighted with the hydrogen of its waters, and its cinders not wholly deprived of their bitumen?

But we are driven to the necessity of believing that Jupiter and the exterior planets are either *water* or *ice*. That they are neither composed of the one material nor the other, is proved by direct experiment. If their surfaces were either wholly or partly aqueous, the rays reflected from them when the planets are in quadrature, would contain, what it does not, a large portion of polarized light; and if their crust consisted of mountains, and precipices, and rocks of ice, some of whose faces must occasionally reflect the incident light at nearly the polarizing angle, the polarization of their light would be distinctly indicated.

Had our author not exhibited the great amount of his knowledge,—an amount so massive as occasionally to smother his reason, we should have charged him with ignorance of the various forms and conditions of density, in which the same elements may be combined; but we believe that he knows these as well as we do, and, in our position, would use them more skilfully. It is difficult to understand why Jupiter should be made of water. His density is 1·359, (that of the Earth being 5·66, and that of water being 1·000,) greater even than that of certain specimens of *coal*, far greater than *amianthus*, and *pumice stone*, which are lighter than water. *Silex* or *flint*, too, occurs with such various densities that there are conditions of it less dense than Jupiter. In the state of *tabasheer* it is very much lighter than water. In the state of *siliceous sinter* its density is only 1·8. In the state of *opal* its density is 1·9, and in certain varieties of *quartz* it is so high as 2·88. There are *pitchstones*, too, varying from 1·9 of specific gravity to 2·70 ; so that the hardest mineral may exist in *Jupiter*, and yet his density not exceed 1·359. But why should the minerals in Jupiter be of the same nature as those on the Earth ? May not the elementary atoms of matter be there combined according to different laws, and form *spars*, and *gems*, and *metals*, entirely different from ours ? Admitting, however, for a moment, the supposition, otherwise inadmissible, that there is a terrestrial type of inorganic bodies which is to be the exemplar for all the planets, we have only to suppose these planets to be hollow, or to contain large cavities, in order to reconcile their average densities with the densities of terrestrial bodies.

The arguments against Saturn being inhabited, our author considers to be much stronger than in the case of Jupiter. He tells us that "the outer part of the globe of Saturn is *proved* to be vapour by his streaks and belts," and that "*we must* either suppose that he has no inhabitants, or that *they are aqueous gelatinous creatures, too sluggish almost to be deemed alive*, floating in their ice cold water, and shrouded for ever by their humid skies!" He "cannot tell us," he says, "whether they have eyes or no, but *probably* if they had, they would never see the sun; and therefore," he continues, "we need not *commiserate their lot* in not seeing the host of Saturnian satellites, and the ring which to an intelligent Saturnian spectator would be so splendid a celestial object. The ring is a glorious object for man's view and his contemplation, and therefore *is not* altogether without its use. Still less need we (as some[1] appear to do) regard as a *serious misfortune* to the inhabitants of certain regions of the planet, a solar eclipse of fifteen years' duration, to which they are liable by the interposition of the ring between them and the sun." This specimen of our author's dialectics, in which a large dose of banter and ridicule is seasoned, with a little condiment of science, forms a painful contrast with the following noble passage, in which Sir John Herschel discusses the very same subject. "The rings of Saturn must present a magnificent spectacle from those regions of the planets which lie above their enlightened sides, as vast arches spanning the sky from horizon to horizon, and holding an almost invariable situation among the stars. On the other hand, in the regions beneath the dark side, a solar eclipse of fifteen years in duration, under their shadow, must afford (to our ideas) an inhospitable asylum to animated beings, ill compensated by the faint light of the satellites. *But we shall do wrong* to judge

[1] The author here refers to Sir John Herschel, whose authority he quotes for the Solar eclipse of fifteen years.—*Outlines, &c.*, § 522.

of the fitness or unfitness of their condition from what we see around us,. when perhaps the very combinations which only convey images of horror to our minds, *may be, in reality, theatres of the most striking and glorious displays of beneficent contrivance.*"

The remarkable phenomenon, however, of a *fifteen* years' eclipse of the sun to the regions of Saturn, placed under the shadow of the dark side of the ring, does not exist. Dr. Lardner, in an elaborate memoir, On the Appearance of Saturn's Rings to the Inhabitants of the Planet,[1] has solved the problem of the appearance of the system of rings in the Saturnian firmament, and their effect in eclipsing occasionally and temporarily the sun, the eight moons, and other celestial objects.

"It is there demonstrated," he says, "that the infinite skill of the great Architect of the universe has not permitted that this stupendous annular appendage, the uses of which still remain undiscovered, should be the cause of such darkness and desolation to the inhabitants of the planet, and such an aggravation of the rigours

1 *Transactions of the Astronomical Society,* 1853, vol. xxii.

of their fifteen years' winter, as it has been inferred to be. . . . . It is shewn, on the contrary, that by the apparent motion of the heavens, produced by the diurnal rotation of Saturn, the celestial objects, including, of course, the sun and the eight moons, are not carried parallel to the edges of the rings, as has been hitherto supposed; that they are moved so as to pass alternately from side to side of each of these edges; that, in general, such objects as pass under the rings are only occulted by them for short intervals, before and after their meridional culmination; that though under some rare and exceptional circumstances and conditions, certain objects, the sun being among the number, are occulted from rising to setting, the continuance of such phenomena is not such as has been supposed, and the places of its occurrence are far more limited. In short, *it has no such character as would deprive the planet of any essential condition of habitability.*"

By arguments "of the same kind, as in the case of Jupiter and Saturn, but greatly increased in strength," as he alleges, our Essayist banishes inhabitants from *Neptune* and *Uranus*, and he sneeringly "commends the supposition of the probable watery nature and low vitality of their inhabitants to the consideration of those who contend for inhabitants in those remote regions of the Solar system."

In returning towards the sun, our author pays his passing respects to *Mars*, which he thinks is more likely to have inhabitants than any other planet. This probability, however, disappears, and he concedes to this planet the possibility of having "creatures of the nature of corals and molluscs, saurians and iguanodons."

The twenty-nine asteroids between Mars and Jupiter afford our author a new and inviting field for speculation. He considers them as *mere dots*, whose form is not even known to be spherical. Setting aside the theory that they are the fragments of an exploded planet, he thinks "they may be the results of some *imperfectly effected* concentration of the elements of our system (of star dust,) which if it had gone on more completely and regularly, might have produced another planet between Mars and Jupiter. Perhaps they are only the larger masses among a great number of smaller ones, resulting from such a process: and it is very conceivable that the meteoric stones, which have from time to time fallen upon the Earth's surface, are other results of the like process;—bits of planets *which have failed in the making, and lost their way* till arrested by the resistance of the Earth's atmosphere!"

The two interior planets, *Venus* and *Mercury*, are depopulated in a single page. The light and heat of Venus is admitted to be only "double those which come to the Earth." He finds it "hard to say what kind of animals he could place in her, except perhaps the microscopic creatures with siliceous coverings, which, as modern explorers assert, are almost indestructible by heat."—"Of Mercury," he says, "we know still less, and he has not, so far as we can tell, any of the conditions which make animal existence conceivable." Opinions of a very different nature from these we have already had occasion to state in a preceding chapter, and we must leave it to the judgment of the reader to decide upon their relative probabilities.

In order to combine under one general principle the views which he has taken of the condition of the individual planets, the Essayist adopts the *nebular hypothesis*, in which the Sun and all the planets are formed out of star dust or fire-mist, by its gradual contraction and the subsequent solidification of its parts, without any interference on the part of the Almighty. Upon this hypothesis he erects a scheme or a theory of the Solar system, which he considers as having a sort of *religious dignity*, though he fears that, at first, it may appear, to many, rash, fanciful, and almost irreverent. In this scheme, the *fire* and *water* of the nebular mass have been separated during their "*planet-making powers*," "the water and the vapour which belong to the system being driven off into the outer regions of its vast circuit, while the solid masses, ... such as result from the fusion of the most solid materials, lie nearer the Sun, and are found principally within the orbit of Jupiter." In support of these theories he adduces the zodiacal light, itself a creature of theory, as an appendage to the Sun, and as the remains of the Sun's atmosphere extending beyond the orbits of Mercury and Venus—"planets which have not yet fully emerged from the atmosphere in which they had their origin—the *mother light* and *mother fire* in which they began to crystallize, as crystals do in their mother water!" These planets are, therefore, within a nebular region, which *may easily be conceived to be uninhabitable.* And where this nebular region, marked by the zodiacal light, terminates, *the world of life begins, namely, at the Earth!* "*The orbit of the Earth is the temperate zone of the Solar system,* and in that zone is the play of Hot and Cold, of Moist and Dry possible."

With these wild and extravagant notions our author connects the shooting stars or meteors which appear in such numbers in our atmosphere. He considers them as "revolving specks of nebulæ," the "outriders of the zodiacal light," which, when "broken into patches, are seen as stars for the moment we are near to them."—"And if this be true," he continues, "we have to correct, in a certain way, what we have previously said of the zodiacal light: that no one had thought of resolving it into stars;

for it would thus appear, that in its outer region *it resolves itself into stars, visible, though but for a moment, to the naked eye!*"

In concluding this novel and startling theory of the Solar system, the Essayist tells us that "the Earth is placed in that region of the system in which the *planet-forming powers* are the most vigorous and potent;—that *the Earth is really the largest planetary body in the Solar system,—its domestic hearth, and the only world in the universe.*"[1] We are unwilling to charge the author of such theories with cherishing opinions hostile to religion. We

[1] A very different opinion is stated by Dr. Whewell, in his Bridgewater Treatise. "The view of the universe," says he, "expands also on another side. The Earth, the globular body thus covered with life, is not the only globe in the universe. There are circling about our own Sun six others, so far as we can judge, *perfectly analogous in their nature:* besides our Moon and other bodies analogous to it. *No one can resist the temptation* to conjecture that these globes, some of them much larger than our own, *are not dead and barren;—that they are, like ours, occupied with organization, life, intelligence.* To conjecture is all that we can do; yet even by the perception of such a possibility, *our view of the kingdom of nature is enlarged and elevated.*"—Chap. ii. pp. 269, 270. The rest of this chapter, "*On the Vastness of the Universe,*"—in which he speaks of the binary systems of the stars as "giving rise possibly to new conditions of worlds,"—of "the millions of stars" in the universe, as containing "the whole range of created objects in our own system,"—and of "the tendency of all the arrangements which we can comprehend to support the existence, develop the faculties, and to promote the happiness of countless species of creature,"—is well worthy of the perusal of the reader, and forms a striking contrast with the opinions of the Essayist.

believe that he is ignorant of their tendency, and that he has forgotten the truths of inspiration, and even those of natural religion, amid the excitement of discussions, from which he is to obtain the high reputation of "having accounted for, and reduced into consistency and connexion, a very extraordinary number of points hitherto unexplained." But, however sincere may be his piety, which we do not question, we tell him, with confidence, that his theories are replete with danger, and that young minds will draw from them opinions the very reverse of his own. When we are told that a planet has been bungled in its formation, that meteoric stones are bits of planets which have failed in the making,[1] and lost their way, can we believe that the all-wise Creator was present at the process, "making the earth by His power, and establishing the world by His wisdom?" Can we believe that He who formed *the worlds* has made only *one*,

[1] "We know of no blemishes or blunders in creation," says Professor Sedgwick, "and were they there, what would it matter to our conception of them, whether they sprang from dead material laws ordained by an all-powerful and all-seeing God, or from an immediate defect in creative power?"

and that, in place of resting on the seventh day, He rested during the whole week of creation, and still rests, having transferred His almighty power to certain laws of matter and motion, by which the Sun and all his planets were *manufactured* from nebulous matter? Sir Isaac Newton considered the nebular theory, though in his time not known by that name, as not only absurd, but verging on atheism. In reference to the creation of a central and immovable sun, he observes, that to suppose a "central particle so accurately placed in the middle (of nebulous matter in a finite space) as to be always equally attracted on all sides, and thereby continue without motion, seems to me fully as hard as to make the sharpest needle stand upright on its point upon a looking-glass. And much harder it is to suppose that all the particles in an infinite space should be so accurately poised, one upon another, as to stand still in a perfect equilibrium. For I reckon this as hard as to make not one needle only, but an infinite number of them, stand accurately poised upon their points."[1]

[1] *Letter to Bentley*, Lett. iv.

And in another place he urges another objection to the hypothesis: "But how the matter (the nebular matter) should divide itself into two sorts, and that part of it which is fit to compose a shining body should fall down into one mass, and make a sun, and the rest, which is fit to compose an opaque body, should coalesce, not into one great body, like the shining matter, but into many little ones, I do not think explicable by mere natural causes, but am forced to ascribe it to the counsel and contrivance of a voluntary agent."[1] And with respect to the diurnal rotation of the planets, he distinctly declares that "they could not be derived from gravity, but required a divine arm to impress them."[2]

A more modern, and still living author, who, we trust, will long continue an honour to science and to his country, has characterized speculations like these, as "dashing from hypothesis to hypothesis, and building a scheme of nature against nature, and against the sober interpretation of those who have best studied their works." We will not say of the language of the

[1] *Letter to Bentley*, Lett. i. [2] *Id.* Lett. iv.

Essayist, when he speaks of Nature, or the God of Nature, having failed in producing a planet where He intended it to be, and of having recorded that failure by broken planets and showers of meteoric stones;[1]—we will not say what Professor Sedgwick has said of speculations about the nebular theory not more absurd, that they are "the raving madness of hypothetical extravagance;" but we sincerely, and without desiring to give offence, adopt the rest of his declaration, "that it is at open war with all the calm lessons of inductive truth, and, in any interpretation we can give it, bears upon its front the stamp of folly and irreverence towards the God of Nature."

"Though this Earth," says Dr. Chalmers, "and these heavens were to disappear, there are other worlds which roll afar;—the light of other suns shines upon them, and the sky which mantles them is garnished with other stars. Is it presumption to say that the moral

[1] "The planets and the stars," says the Essayist, "are the lumps which have flown from the Potter's wheel of the Great-worker, the shred coils of which, in His working, sprung from His mighty lathe;—the sparks which darted from His awful anvil, when the Solar system lay incandescent thereon;—the curls of vapour which rose from the great cauldron of creation, when its elements were separated."—P. 243.

world extends to these distant and unknown regions; that they are occupied with people; that the charities of home and of neighbourhood flourish there; that the praises of God are there lifted up, and His goodness rejoiced in; that piety has there its temples and its offerings; and that the richness of the Divine attributes is there felt and admired by intelligent worshippers?"[1]

[1] *Astronomical Discourses*, pp. 36, 37.—Without multiplying extracts from the writings of philosophers and divines, it may be sufficient to state, that Dr. Derham, in his *Astrotheology*, 3d edit., 1717, pp. xlvii., liii., liv., has stated his reasons for believing that the fixed stars and planets "are *worlds*, or places of *habitation*, which is concluded from their being *habitable*, and well provided for *habitation*." Dr. Paley also, though he does not discuss the subject, evinces his opinion when he states, "that even ignorance of the *sensitive* natures *by which other planets are inhabited*, necessarily keeps from us the knowledge of numberless utilities, relations, and subserviences, which we perceive upon our own globe."—*Natural Theology*, edited by Lord Brougham and Sir Charles Bell, London, 1836, p. 16.

CHAPTER XV.

THE FUTURE OF THE UNIVERSE.

HAD the doctrine of a Plurality of Worlds been one of those subjects which merely gratify our curiosity, we should not have occupied the reader's time, or spent our own, in illustrating and defending it. While the scientific truths on which it depends form one of the most interesting branches of natural theology, and yield the most striking proofs of wisdom and design, they are intimately associated with the future destiny of Man.

There are three departments of Natural Theology which demand our most earnest attention, —the living world around us, the world of the past, and the worlds of the future. In the wonderful mechanisms of animal and vegetable life with which we are so familiar, and in the inorganic structures amid which we dwell, we recognise imperfectly the innumerable proofs of matchless skill and benevolent adaptations with which they abound. Our daily familiarity with the ordinary functions of life, degrades them in our estimation. There is something which we deem unclean even in the healthy condition of animal bodies, and their functions and their products, which deters all but professional men from their study, and robs them of their inherent claims as incentives to piety, and as proofs of design. Even the chemistry of inspiration by which we live, and the science of the Eye and the Ear, on which all our intercourse with nature and with society depends, are scarcely known to the best educated of the people.

It is otherwise, however, with that department of natural science which treats of the formations and fossil remains of an ancient world. With the structure and functions of animals which inhabited the earth previous to its occupation by man, we have no familiarity. We see them only in their graves of stone, and beneath their monuments of marble—creations which cannot again die, and with which every thing mortal has ceased to be associated. Time, in its most hoary aspect, has invested them with a hallowed and a mystic character. The green waves have washed them in their coral beds, and after ages of ablution in a tempestuous sea, the ordeal of a central fire has completed their purification. The bones, and the integuments, and the meanest products of animal life, have thus become sainted relics which the most sensitive may handle, and the most delicate may prize.

But there is another department of natural science which in its interests, is deeper and more varied still. Carrying us back to the birth of matter, before life was breathed among its atoms, and before light rushed through the darkness of space, Astronomy unites, in a remarkable degree, the interests of the past, the present, and the future. From the time when the Earth was without form and void to the present hour, Astronomy has been the study of the shepherd and the sage, and in the bosom of sidereal space the genius of man has explored the most gigantic works of the Almighty, and studied the most mysterious of His arrangements. But while the astronomer ponders over the wonderful structures of the spheres, and investigates the laws of their movements, the Christian contemplates them with a warmer and more affectionate interest. From their past and present history his eager eye turns to the future of the sidereal systems, and he looks to them as the hallowed spots in which his immortal existence is to run. Scripture has not spoken with an articulate voice of the future locality of the blest, but Reason has combined the scattered utterances of Inspiration, and with a voice, almost oracular, has declared that He who made the worlds, will in the worlds which He has made, place the beings of His choice. In the spiritual character of their faith, the ambassadors of our Saviour have not referred to the materiality of His future kingdom; but Reason compels us to believe, that the material body, which is to be raised, must be subject to material laws, and reside in a material home—a house of many mansions, though not made with many hands.

In what regions of space these mansions are built—on what sphere the mouldering dust is to be gathered and revived, and by what process it is to reach its destination, reason does not enable us to determine; but it is impossible for immortal man, with the light of revelation as his guide, to doubt for a moment that on the celestial spheres his future is to be spent—spent, doubtless, in lofty inquiries—in social intercourse—in the renewal of domestic ties,—and in the service of his almighty Benefactor. With such a vista before us, so wide in its expanse, and so remote in its termination, what scenes of beauty—what forms of the sublime—what enjoyments, physical and intellectual, may we not anticipate,—wisdom to the sage—rest to the pilgrim—and gladness to the broken in heart!

> "How welcome those untrodden spheres!
> How sweet this very hour to die!
> To soar from earth, and find all fears
> Lost in thy light—Eternity.
>
> "Oh! in that future let us think
> To hold each heart the heart that shares;
> With them the immortal waters drink,
> And soul in soul grow deathless theirs."—BYRON.

If these expectations are just, how are we to implant them in the popular mind as incentives to piety and principles of action? The future of the Christian is not defined in his creed. Enwrapt in apocalyptic mysteries, it evades his grasp, and presents no salient points upon which either reason or imagination can rest. He looks beyond the grave as into a nebular region, where a few stars are with difficulty descried; but he sees no glorious suns, and no gorgeous planets upon which he is to dwell. It is astronomy alone, when its simple truths are impressed upon the mind, that opens to the Christian's eye the mysterious expanse of the universe; that fills it with objects which arrest his deepest attention; and that creates an intelligible paradise in the world to come. We must, therefore, impregnate the popular mind with the truths of natural science, teaching them in every school, and recommending, if not illustrating them, from every pulpit. We must instruct our youth, and even age itself, in the geology and physical geography of the globe, that they may thus learn the structure and use of its brother planets; and we must fix in their memories, and associate with their affections, the great truths in the planetary and sidereal universe on which the doctrine of more worlds than one must necessarily rest. Thus familiar with the great works of creation,—thus seeing them through the heart, as well as through the eye, the young will look to the future with a keener glance, and with brighter hopes ;—the weary and the heavy laden will rejoice in the vision of their place of rest ;—the philosopher will scan with a new sense the lofty spheres in which he is to study ;—and the Christian will recognise, in the eternal abodes, the gorgeous Temples in which he is to offer his sacrifice of praise.

For EU product safety concerns, contact us at Calle de José Abascal, 56–1°, 28003 Madrid, Spain or eugpsr@cambridge.org.

www.ingramcontent.com/pod-product-compliance
Ingram Content Group UK Ltd.
Pitfield, Milton Keynes, MK11 3LW, UK
UKHW010343140625
459647UK00010B/789

* 9 7 8 1 1 0 8 0 0 4 1 6 9 *